AF326571

Ritual and Christian Worship

Ritual and Christian Worship

Jeffrey A. Truscott

CASCADE *Books* · Eugene, Oregon

RITUAL AND CHRISTIAN WORSHIP

Copyright © 2023 Jeffrey A. Truscott. All rights reserved. Except for brief quotations in critical publications or reviews, no part of this book may be reproduced in any manner without prior written permission from the publisher. Write: Permissions, Wipf and Stock Publishers, 199 W. 8th Ave., Suite 3, Eugene, OR 97401.

Cascade Books
An Imprint of Wipf and Stock Publishers
199 W. 8th Ave., Suite 3
Eugene, OR 97401

www.wipfandstock.com

PAPERBACK ISBN: 978-1-5326-8689-4
HARDCOVER ISBN: 978-1-5326-8690-0
EBOOK ISBN: 978-1-5326-8691-7

Cataloguing-in-Publication data:

Names: Truscott, Jeffrey A., author.

Title: Ritual and Christian worship / by Jeffrey A. Truscott.

Description: Eugene, OR: Cascade Books, 2023 | Includes bibliographical references and index.

Identifiers: ISBN 978-1-5326-8689-4 (paperback) | ISBN 978-1-5326-8690-0 (hardcover) | ISBN 978-1-5326-8691-7 (ebook)

Subjects: LCSH: Ritualism. | Ritual. | Rites and ceremonies. | Sacraments.

Classification: BV185.T20 2023 (print) | BV185 (ebook)

01/03/23

All Scripture quotations, unless otherwise stated, are taken from the Holy Bible New International Version®, NIV®. Copyright © 1973, 1978, 1984, 2011 by Biblica, Inc.™ Used by permission of Zondervan. All rights reserved worldwide. www.zondervan.com

Contents

Abbreviations

<table>
<tr><td>AL</td><td>The Annotated Luther. 6 vols. Edited by Hans Hillerbrand et al. Minneapolis: Fortress, 2015–17.</td></tr>
<tr><td>BC</td><td>The Book of Concord. Edited by Robert Kolb and Timothy J. Wengert. Minneapolis: Fortress, 2000.</td></tr>
<tr><td>CTT</td><td>Calvin: Theological Treatises. Edited and translated by J. K. S. Reid. Vol. 22 of The Library of Christian Classics. Edited and translated by J. K. S. Reid. Louisville: Westminster John Knox, 2006.</td></tr>
<tr><td>DLW</td><td>The New SCM Dictionary of Liturgy and Worship. Edited by Paul F. Bradshaw. London: SCM, 2002.</td></tr>
<tr><td>DTHS</td><td>New Dictionary of Theology Historical and Systematic. 2nd ed. Downers Grove, IL: InterVarsity, 2016.</td></tr>
<tr><td>ELW</td><td>Evangelical Lutheran Worship. Minneapolis: Augsburg Fortress, 2006.</td></tr>
<tr><td>ISBD</td><td>The International Standard Bible Dictionary. Rev. ed. Grand Rapids: Eerdmans, 1988.</td></tr>
<tr><td>LW</td><td>Luther's Works [American edition]. 82 vols. planned. Edited by Jaroslav Pelikan et al. Philadelphia: Fortress; St. Louis: Concordia, 1955–1986; 2009—.</td></tr>
<tr><td>NBD</td><td>New Bible Dictionary. 3rd ed. Downers Grove, IL: InterVarsity, 1996.</td></tr>
</table>

PW   Evangelical Lutheran Church in America. *Principles for Worship.* Minneapolis: Augsburg Fortress, 2002.

UMG   Evangelical Lutheran Church in America. *Use of the Means of Grace: A Statement on the Practice of Word and Sacrament.* Minneapolis: Augsburg Fortress, 1997.

WA   *Luthers Werke: Kritische Gesamtausgabe [Schriften].* 65 vols. Weimar: H. Böhlau, 1883–1953.

WDB   *The New Westminster Dictionary of the Bible.* Edited by Henry S. Gehman. Philadelphia: Westminster, 1970.

Introduction

In my last book, *Twelve Whys of Worship* (2018), I attempted to explain why Christians do what we do in our services of public worship: Why do we pray? Why do we sing? Why do we confess our sins? The objective was to help Christians become informed planners and participants in the Sunday service of Word and sacrament. This book was well-received here in Singapore, and it became the basis of public lectures that I gave. Yet I perceived that something more needed to be said. While I explained the theological significance of the various acts of Christian worship, I had not explained why the Sunday service involves patterned, repetitive acts in the first place! Why not just gather to listen to a sermon and then meditate silently? Why organize time, space, and objects, and employ stylized gestures and movements in order to immerse ourselves in the divine truths that form us into Christians? Why keep on doing these things week after week? So the task, then, was to explain *ritual*.

While there are many volumes on ritual by cultural anthropologists and ritual studies experts, there are comparatively few works on ritual for general audiences by liturgical theologians or historians. Thus, the purpose of this book is to explore ritual and its place in Christian worship, and to provide something of a user's guide for leaders and planners of worship. In explaining ritual objectively and winsomely, this book will serve as an apologetic; in seeking to guide liturgical performance, it will be practical.

While thoroughly historical and theological, this book is also anthropological in that it draws on the insights of certain human sciences. Readers should note that it is impossible to talk about ritual without referring to these. But this is not a book on ritual theory, nor is it a theology of ritual. I write as a historian of the liturgy asking questions about ritual and the liturgy, wondering not only why liturgy is ritualized, but what the Christian tradition has to say about ritual *as* ritual. At the same time, I write as a pastor concerned about the practice of the liturgy and its various rituals. It seems to me that if we cannot understand ritual and be comfortable with it, liturgical practice will be marked by uncertainty, nervousness, and attempts to transform the liturgy into something with which we are comfortable—education, entertainment, or a program of personal improvement. Thus, my hope is that this book will help readers get comfortable in their own ritual skins.

As an introduction, chapter 1 will define key terms: *ritual, ritualization, symbol,* and *sign.* It will also provide a brief overview of ritual in the life and worship of the church. Chapter 2 surveys the insights of life sciences concerning the origins of ritual and the relationship between the human body and ritual. The reader will come to appreciate how religious experience is the product of ritual actions that necessarily use the body. To help us further understand how ritual utilizes various aspects of the human world to speak spiritual truth, chapter 3 explores the components of ritual. Ritual uses elements of culture such as song, dance, and storytelling, and organizes space, time, and human relationships in order to form religious affections in the participants. Chapter 4 will consider how ritual was vital to the life and worship of ancient Israel and to early Christianity. It will demonstrate that religious life is centered on ritual. Of course, this does not mean that prophetic voices cannot and do not raise concerns about ritual matters. Reform of liturgical ritual was at the top of the agendas of Martin Luther and John Calvin, and their thinking about ritual is the subject of our penultimate chapter (5). While both of these theologians profoundly criticized the ritual practices of their day, they also appreciated the role of ritual and ceremony in disciplining and forming the faith of Christians. Their nuanced and balanced positions on ritual, I believe, can speak to the church today. As a kind of summary, chapter 6 lays out principles for the practice of ritual, drawing particularly on the previous chapter. It is hoped that worship leaders of all liturgical traditions will find these principles useful.

Finally, I wish to express my thanks to the following: Cascade Books for agreeing to take up this project; Matthew Wimer for his assistance as editor; Rev. Dr. Frank C. Senn (USA) and Mr. Png Eng Keat (Singapore) for reading and commenting on draft chapters; Trinity Theological College, Singapore, for allowing me to continue to live and work here during the

COVID-19 pandemic which, unfortunately, delayed my move to Sekolah Tinggi Theologia, Pematangsiantar, Indonesia, where I have been called to teach homiletics and liturgics. All of these have my deepest gratitude for their support during the writing of this book.

xi

Jeffrey A. Truscott

October 2021
Singapore

Chapter 1

What Is Ritual?

Thinking about "Ritual"

ALTHOUGH THIS IS A book about ritual and Christian worship, it must be stated at the very beginning that ritual is not limited to overtly religious doings. Important life activities revolve around routines, customs, and habits. Eating is a communal action subject to customs involving posture, the use of utensils, and the appropriate words to say before and after eating. In most societies, the acts of greeting and taking leave of others have customary words and gestures. The manner of speech used when addressing older versus younger people or when speaking to those who belong to one's social group versus those who do not are likewise set by custom.

Group life can involve customs, habits, and routines that are specific to a group. Family life has its regular gatherings for meals, reunions with members of the extended family, and celebrations of birthdays and wedding anniversaries. Life as a student at school requires people to routinely wear a uniform, assemble for the raising of the school flag, and sing the school anthem. Sporting events include customary activities, such as cheering (using a set of prescribed words) and wearing clothing with the team's colors. Civic life is punctuated with regular observances such as a national or independence day, with its parades, speeches, and the singing of well-known patriotic songs. The civic calendar will also include days for remembering national heroes, the war dead, and important historical events.

As for the Christian church, customs and habits apart from public worship services make up its life. Local churches have set times for their annual general meetings to discuss business and elect leadership. There might be a yearly "church camp" for instruction, recreation, and group-building activities. Small groups meet at stated times each week for informal prayer, Bible study, and fellowship. Like all people, Christians usually engage in routines without thinking that what they are doing is ritual. Indeed, people in general do not consider the routines and customs of life as rituals.

When it comes to ritual in public worship, Protestants have been especially wary, partly due to historical reasons. The Reformers of the sixteenth century rejected many rituals that they considered unbiblical and superstitious. Later the Enlightenment's denial of any supernatural power in liturgical rites led to a devaluation of ritual in general. Consequently, many contemporary Protestant churches are concerned about ritual acts becoming "empty" and "meaningless," and accordingly limit the number of ritual acts in public worship and emphasize the verbal over the visual and tactile.

But Christians in the late twentieth century began to rethink the place of ritual in the church and its public worship. This development owes to the research of social scientists who treat ritual as a normal part of human existence. Rather than attacking or defending ritual, these researchers have sought to explain the reasons for its existence and its role in human society. Arguably, their work can help us to understand ritual and how we might more effectively use it in worship.

Toward a Definition of "Ritual"

For sure, the objectivity and neutrality of social scientists on the matter of ritual can be helpful. One theologian influenced by the social science approach to ritual is the Lutheran liturgical scholar Frank C. Senn, who defines ritual as "a pattern of behavior that expresses and forms a way of life consistent with the community's beliefs and values."[1] This definition of ritual applies equally to actions in the church as well as to those in the broader society. We should note that "ritual" is a general concept that encompasses different types of actions such as speech, song, movement, drama, etc., while "rite" is a specific instance of ritual, e.g., the rite of baptism.[2] But not all patterned and repeated actions are rituals. Since it has no reference to communal beliefs, nor forms people in the ways of a community, an action like brushing one's teeth is not an instance of ritual.

Let us now unpack Senn's definition. The phrase "pattern of behavior" reminds us that ritual involves actions that a community turns to repeatedly because there is a shared understanding that these actions mean

1. Senn, *Christian Liturgy*, 3.
2. Mitchell, "Rite, Ritual," 407.

certain things or have particular functions. For example, the church makes new Christians by washing the candidates while speaking the name of the triune God. Because this action is part of our common understanding and experience, we know what it is every time we see it and we know that its recipient has become a Christian. Because baptism involves a pattern of actions known and understood by the whole community, there is no need to reinvent the wheel every time that we want to initiate a person into our fellowship. In that case, rituals promote order and efficiency.

The second half of the definition, "expresses and forms a way of life," means that ritual not only conveys ideas but is meant to change the way people think and live. Formation through ritual, however, is not only verbal, but is also visual and tactile—a holistic experience, which is preferable. The best way to teach a particular swimming stroke is to verbally explain it while the student is in the swimming pool and can emulate the actions of the instructor and thus "get a feel" for the stroke. By allowing our active participation through sight, sound, smell, and even taste, ritual enables spiritual truth to be perceived at a deeper level and to be retained in memory. Participation through bodily action essentially stores memory in the body, such that the body remembers how to perform an action (like how to ride a bicycle), and every use of the body in a particular ritual action will evoke the memories, beliefs, and affections associated with the action. It is no wonder that singing, which requires the use of the entire body, has been an important ritual activity for Christianity and other faith communities.

"Consistent with the community's beliefs and values" means that ritual is bound up with a community's most deeply held affirmations about God and the relationship of the community with God. Through ritual, beliefs are *acted out* (or "enacted"). Believing that becoming a Christian means the death of a former self and the raising up of a new person, Christians plunge a person under water—nearly drowning him or her!—and then pull the person out of the water, saving the person from drowning. Baptism ritually enacts what we believe conversion means. But we also believe that it effects this reality in the believer through the work of the Holy Spirit. Believing that Jesus Christ and his sacrificial death are nourishment for hungry souls, we hold a sacred meal in memory of him. The Lord's Supper enacts ritually what we believe about Christ. But we also hold that this very meal imparts the nourishment that is Christ, because it offers participation in his body and blood (1 Cor 10:16).

As the above examples of "death and resurrection" and "spiritual nourishment" demonstrate, Christians, like people of other faiths, deal in realities that are difficult to express except through rituals that reference common actions and images, like eating and bathing. It would be difficult to "do" the Christian faith other than through rituals, or as Senn puts it, there is no "unritualized Christian life."[3] Accordingly, nearly all churches have ritual, even those that are on the opposite end of the ritual spectrum from the so-called "liturgical" or "traditional" churches. Although rejecting the traditional sacraments, the Salvation Army still has a rite for the making of new "soldiers," namely a "swearing in ceremony" under the Army's trinitarian flag, followed by the signing of the "Articles of War."[4] Even the Society of Friends (aka the Quakers), which rejects *all* ritual acts, has a regular public gathering ("meeting") or liturgy that expresses its beliefs about God and is meant for ongoing formation of society members.[5]

The main differences among churches are the number of rituals used and the degree to which rituals are controlled by formal sets of rules known as rubrics. The so-called liturgical churches (e.g., Lutheran, Anglican), who out of a discriminating conservatism, retained many of the liturgical rites of the medieval church, have larger bodies of rites than those churches that developed later in history and mostly rejected the traditional rites. The differentiation in formality among churches is evident in prayer. In some traditions, the opening prayer of a service might be prayed spontaneously by the minister, with little more structure than the common understanding that this prayer should express the adoration of God. In other Christian traditions (e.g., Luther and Anglican), the opening *collect prayer* for the service, usually taken from a prayer book, follows a stylized pattern: opening address to God, ascription of some attribute of God, request, result of request, and concluding formula. Prayer is thus patterned in some manner regardless of the liturgical tradition of the person offering it.

Signs and Symbols

Ritual uses signs and symbols to express and impart meaning. A *sign* is a means of representation in which one thing points to another thing. For example, a red, octagonal sign with the word "STOP" printed in the

3. Senn, *Christian Liturgy*, 4.

4. Rightmire, "Salvation Army Worship," 421.

5. Anderson, "Quaker Worship," 395.

center represents the need for a driver to bring her car to a halt on the road. *Symbols*, a subcategory of signs, do not simply convey meaning, but give heightened or new meaning by helping us to understand A in terms of B. Language is one place where we can see this expansion of meaning taking place. If someone withholds important information from others, we say that she "kept them in the dark." In this case, "darkness" is held up against a situation where people were left unaware or uninformed, just like one might be unaware of dangers when walking down an unlighted pathway. The symbolic language brings together two realities and thereby enables the mind's eye to "see" the truth of a particular situation.

The word *symbol* comes from the Greek *symballein*, which literally means "to throw together." In the ancient Greek context, two parties in a contract would cut an object in two. Although the two pieces were meaningless in and of themselves, when brought together they "symbolized" the contract between the two individuals and identified each person as a party to the contract. By bringing about an expansion of meaning (or by generating new meaning) symbols appeal to the imagination, creating an "aha!" moment in our minds. It is nearly impossible to express abstract, spiritual concepts except by the creation of new meaning through the symbolic juxtaposition of images and concepts.

As the above example of a contract suggests, symbols are related to identity. The flag of a nation is a sign because it represents a particular geographical place and political entity. But it is also a symbol because by evoking memories and values it gives people an identity, that is, a symbol is a way for people to participate in what it means (for example) to be a Singaporean or a Malaysian. Indeed, identification with a particular flag is a way of being a citizen of a particular country. Similarly, a wedding ring is a sign of the marital relationship between a man and a woman, but it becomes a symbol insofar as the wearing of the wedding ring is one of the ways that a person participates in the marital relationship, since the ring confirms one's identity as a spouse and evokes the memory of the marriage vow. Precisely because the wedding ring is about participation and identity, a person might become upset if his/her spouse loses the wedding ring, since the very object that is bound up with the marital relationship is no longer in sight to symbolize that relationship.

In the New Testament, we can see the relationship between ritual and symbol. In Romans 6, Paul speaks of baptism in terms of a death and resurrection, or more precisely, the Christian's participation in Christ's death and resurrection. The image is meant to suggest what it means to live as someone who has left behind an old life opposed to God (i.e., died to sin) and now lives as a true follower of Jesus Christ (having been raised to a life of righteousness). Thus, for Paul, baptism signifies conversion and a change of life, yet for him it also seems to be the very means of participating in that new life. Indeed, the reference in Titus 3 to baptism as a "washing of new birth and renewal by the Holy Spirit" (v. 5) suggests that the rite of baptism is intimately connected with a new spiritual reality.

Symbols and symbolism also come into play in the Lord's Supper. In the story of the Supper's institution (Matt 26:26–29; Mark 14:22–25; Luke 22:15–20; cf. 1 Cor 11:23–26) Jesus speaks symbolically about the bread that he shares with his disciples ("this is my body"). The identification of the bread with Jesus' body means that, at one level, the bread of the Lord's Supper is a sign, in the sense that it points to or represents the body of Christ that was handed over to death for us. But for Paul, the bread is a symbol in that it offers participation in the reality of Jesus who suffered for humanity's sake (1 Cor 10:16). Thus, the Supper, as a symbol, is a way or experiencing the presence of the risen Lord and knowing ourselves as his redeemed people.

The above examples of baptism and the Lord's Supper highlight the role of natural symbols in ritual. Our rites use food from the earth and the everyday actions of eating and bathing as symbols for how we begin and maintain our relationship with the triune God. In a sense, ritual "meets us where we are" in order to draw us more deeply into a relationship with God. I would suggest that it is only when we appreciate the earthiness and commonness of ritual that we can be good users of it.

Ritual and the Church

Under the broad concept of ritual, we can differentiate and classify rites according to their function in the church. The Romanian historian of religion Mircea Eliade categorized rites according to how they sanctify time, life, and space, i.e., how they relate humans and their world to God and the sacred realm. Rites that sanctify life and life transitions include those for

- Initiation (baptism, confirmation, first reception of Holy Communion)
- Penance (confession and forgiveness)

- Vocation (ordination, comissionings, installations, consecrations)
- Marriage
- Childbirth
- Sickness
- Anniversaries (of marriage, ordination)
- Death and burial

The above are all occasional, that is, they are observed on an "as-needed" basis. Rites for the sanctification of time, which occur in repeating cycles, include

- Daily prayer services
- Weekly services of Word and sacrament
  (i.e., the typical Sunday service)
- Festivals and seasons of the church calendar

Rites for the sanctification of space, which are either occasional or cyclical, include

- Dedication of church buildings; blessings of homes
  and other dwellings
- Homecomings, pilgrimages
- Groundbreaking, anniversaries.[6]

Nearly all churches have rituals for significant life occasions such as anniversaries, and transitions such as sickness. The degree of formality can vary from lengthy rites with prescribed prayers and actions, to no more than extemporaneous prayers. Protestants would agree that life transitions are precarious times and that life-cycle rites serve to bring comfort, assurance, and spiritual direction to people during times of change. By minimizing anxiety, transitional rites enable people to accept and live faithfully in new social roles.

As for rites that sanctify time, some churches (e.g., Anglican and Lutheran) have formal services of daily public prayer, especially in the morning and evening, while other churches may simply encourage members to pray every day at home with family members likewise in the morning and evening. As noted above nearly all Protestant churches have a public service (or

6. Cited in Senn, *Christian Liturgy*, 8.

"liturgy") on Sunday morning in which the sharing of God's Word through Scripture readings and sermons and the celebration of the Lord's Supper (at least occasionally) are the central actions. The observance of time varies, with some churches following complex liturgical calendars that memorialize the life of Christ and various saints, while others make practically no distinctions with regard to times and seasons. Yet almost all churches observe Christmas and Easter, festivals that in some countries have become integrated into the broader culture—at least superficially. Christians agree that the day is to be punctuated with prayer, the week with a public worship gathering (of Word and sacrament), and the year with the remembrance of Christ's life. Thus, rites related to time ground the Christian life in prayer, reflection on God's Word, and in Jesus Christ himself.

As for space, many Protestants would deny that a church building and its environs possess any sacredness in and of themselves. At most they would say that a space or building is set apart because of the actions that take place there, namely, the weekly worship service of Word and sacrament. Most Protestants offer special prayers when ground is broken for the construction of a new building and then later when the building is dedicated—focusing on the fulfillment of the intended purpose of the building. Similarly, many churches have special rites for the dedication of important church furnishings such as pulpits, altar tables, musical instruments, baptismal fonts, and communion vessels. For Protestants, a "homecoming" service that welcomes back members and former members living far away from the church will both pray for these persons and give thanks for the "home" church itself.

Pilgrimages or journeys to places deemed to possess special sacredness is not a well-known concept in Protestantism. Yet in reality many Protestants are going on pilgrimages when they travel to Israel to visit places associated with the life of Jesus (e.g., the Church of the Holy Sepulcher, the Mount of Olives, or the Garden Tomb of Jesus in Jerusalem). The same is true when Christians travel great distances to see theatrical productions that depict the life and passion of Jesus or some other biblical story. In the case of Holy Land tours, the "pilgrims" do not visit sites believing that they are sanctified merely because they set foot on places where the Lord Jesus himself once walked. Rather they believe that the experience enhances their biblical knowledge and thus enhances a faith based on believing in the biblical word. For most Protestants, pilgrimages are occasional, although some pilgrimages might be cyclical if people regularly lead or participate in tours to the Holy Land.

Conclusion

Although "ritual" might be a neuralgic term for some Christians, there is no denying that Christian life is shaped by ritual or ritual experiences. I dare say that it is impossible for any branch of Christianity to avoid or transcend ritual, given the symbolic nature of religion in general and of Christianity in particular. But before we can say anything about ritual in Christian worship, we have to ask why ritual is part of human life at all. The starting point for such an inquiry is the life sciences, and so the following chapter will consider what some of these disciplines have to say about ritual.

Chapter 2

Ritual as Studied in the Life Sciences

Introduction

THIS CHAPTER IS AN introduction to ritual and the body from the perspective of the life sciences. The first two areas covered—brain science and ethology—enable us to appreciate ritual as an innate part of human existence, as opposed to being a special activity that only religious people engage in. The other two areas, anthropology and performance theory, help us to understand the transformative nature of ritual. Thus, in this chapter we will explore the development of ritual in human life as well as its function for communities and individuals. Because each of the above listed disciplines could fill volumes with its insights about ritual, this chapter can offer no more than a brief summary of a few key works. The hope is that the reader will be led to think more deeply about ritual and be inspired to do further reading in these areas.

Brain Science, Biology, and Evolution

Recent decades have seen a rise of interest in the relationship between biology and religion. Authors have endeavored to describe how human evolution gave rise to myth and ritual, and how the brain functions in ritual and ritualistic activity. Christians, however, may be concerned that explaining religion in terms of biology and brain function could suggest that God is just "in one's head"—as opposed to God's "existence" being an objective reality beyond the individual. But for many authors, a biological basis of religion and ritual is not opposed to the affirmation that God exists as a transcendent reality. Furthermore, this whole avenue of exploration can

10

help us understand why ritual is an inextricable part of our human existence and of the Christian faith as well.

One recent work devoted to brain science and religion is *Why God Won't Go Away: Brain Science and the Biology of Belief,* by Andrew Newberg, Eugene d'Aquili,[1] and Vince Rause. Referencing various clinical experiments, the authors analyze the inner workings of the brain relative to religious experience. Their starting point is "mystical experience," which they describe as a sense of unity or connectedness with realities beyond one's self. The part of the brain that helps us to differentiate ourselves from other things, the Orientation Association Area (OAA), they note, experiences reduced levels of activity during meditation, such that it is temporarily "blinded." When deprived of information, the OAA is less able to help us distinguish between ourselves and things outside of us—in short, allowing a merger of the self with all other things.[2] This experience of oneness is especially common in the meditation practices of the Eastern mystical tradition, but it was also known by Western mystics, e.g., Angela of Foligno (1248–1309). Newberg and his coauthors argue that the experience of absorption into a larger reality is not merely an emotional state or "wishful thinking," but can be objectively correlated with observable neurological events.[3] In other words, spirituality is bound up with human biology. Far from indicating faulty brain activity, the experience of connecting with transcendent realities and with all other things involves neurological processes.[4]

Newberg and his cohorts identify three areas of the brain that are involved in spiritual experience:

1. For more than forty years, neuroscience has been studying the role of the brain in trance, meditation, mythmaking, and ritual. Psychiatrist Eugene d'Aquili (1940–1998) was a pioneer in this research, publishing several books and numerous articles in this area with his colleagues. He died before the publication of *Why God Won't Go Away,* which was finished by his laboratory partner, Andrew Newberg.

2. Newberg et al., *Why God Won't Go Away,* 6.

3. Newberg et al., *Why God Won't Go Away,* 7. The reader should note that I am somewhat wary of the notion of "absorption" into a greater reality or into the being of God. Such a notion seems to blur the distinction between the Creator and creature, which is of utmost importance in Christian theology. Instead, I prefer to think of the brain's involvement as one of fostering an awareness of God or facilitating an encounter with God.

4. Newberg et al., *Why God Won't Go Away,* 9.

1. The Visual Association Area (VAA), which has a role in visual imagery. The VAA is active when a person uses visual images in meditation, but is also active when there are spontaneous visions during prayer and meditation. It is thought that the visions of those undergoing near-death experiences originate in the VAA. Newberg and company validate this claim based on experiments in which the electrical stimulation of the VAA resulted in vivid visual experiences.[5] The fact that stored visions are remembered and find association with subsequent experiences means that there is an interface with those parts of the brain that have to do with stored memories.[6]

2. The Attention Association Area (AAA), aka the "prefrontal cortex," which controls movements and behaviors related to the attainment of goals and movement toward desired locations. Essentially the "seat of the will," the AAA keeps us "on task" by screening out irrelevant information. There is increased activity in the AAA during religious activities and spiritual experiences. The reason for this is that the AAA is involved in emotional responses, which are part of religious/mystical experience.

3. The Verbal Conceptual Association Area (VCAA), which is involved in the production of abstract concepts and connecting these with particular words, thus enabling us to compare concepts, order opposites, and name objects and categories. It plays a crucial role in our consciousness and the expression of our consciousness through language. It enables us to understand, express, and categorize religious experiences. The VCAA is involved with religious language, icons, and the development of myths. The VCAA has a connection with the frontal lobe of the brain, which is thought to have a role in mythmaking.[7]

Newberg and company note that these brain "areas" are the most highly developed parts of the brain and give us a coherent picture of ourselves and the reality around us. Since different areas of the brain have a connection with different aspects of religious experience, the role of the brain in religious experience must be taken seriously.

Besides the four "areas" of the brain, the autonomic nervous system (ANS), composed of the sympathetic and parasympathetic branches, has

5. Newberg et al., *Why God Won't Go Away*, 27.

6. Newberg et al., *Why God Won't Go Away*, 27.

7. Newberg et al., *Why God Won't Go Away*, 28–31.

a role in mystical/spiritual experience. The sympathetic system controls the body's fight-or-flight response, e.g., making the heart beat faster when engaged, for example, in hunting or battle. Indeed, anything having to do with survival will involve the sympathetic system. By contrast, the parasympathetic system helps the body to maintain equilibrium. It is associated with the regulation of sleep, digestion, and the use of nutrients. These two systems, which might be abbreviated as the "arousal" and "quiescent" systems respectively,[8] function in tandem when there are maximum activity levels during altered states of consciousness—thus suggesting a connection between the ANS and mystical/spiritual experience. Newberg and his co-authors note that there are typically changes in heart and breathing rates, as well as in blood pressure, during yoga and transcendental meditation. They identify four autonomic states that help us to understand and explain the link between the ANS and mystical/spiritual states:

1. Hyperquiescence—a state of unusual relaxation or "complete tranquility" experienced only in sleep or meditation, which can be evoked by ritualistic behaviors such as chanting and group prayer;

2. Hyperarousal—an extraordinary sense of excitement or alertness accompanied by strong concentration, which can be initiated by continuous dancing or other ritualistic behaviors;

3. Hyperquiescence with arousal breakthrough—a state of "bliss" resulting from a quiescent activity, that leads to the activation of the arousal system and a "rush" of energy;

4. Hyperarousal with quiescent breakthrough—essentially the opposite of 3 above, it involves a quiescent "surge" during which there is a trancelike state, making for an experience of ecstasy.[9]

These four states connect the body to the mind, and are related to our emotions, which demonstrates that the ANS has a connection to the limbic system (the part of the brain that "interweaves" emotional impulses and higher thoughts resulting in emotional states like disgust, frustration, anger, and jealousy). Because the stimulation of the limbic system can produce dreamlike states and so-called "out-of-body experiences" and illusions, the limbic system also has a role in religious experiences.[10] Since

8. Newberg et al., *Why God Won't Go Away*, 38–39.

9. Newberg et al., *Why God Won't Go Away*, 40–42.

10. Newberg et al., *Why God Won't Go Away*, 42.

there is an integral relationship between the brain and religious experience, Newberg and company conclude that "if God does indeed exist, the only place he [sic] can manifest his existence would be in the tangled neural pathways and physiological structures of the brain."[11]

The authors of *Why God Won't Go Away* note that the experience of God is bound up with myth—the stories that speak to the deepest emotional and spiritual needs of people by addressing the profound questions and problems of human existence (e.g., our origins, the problems of sin and death, the ultimate destinies of humanity and the universe).[12] Because religion involves the mind and the workings of the brain, the origins of myth are necessarily biological and cognitive.

Like many other authors, Newberg and his colleagues believe that myths are generated in order to alleviate fear and give guidance in the face of dangers. While animals respond to fear with either "fight or flight," humans can think of danger in the abstract, and thus anticipate dangers even when they are not imminent. This is due to the workings of the cerebral cortex, and because the cortex is linked to the limbic system and ANS, the mere thought of danger triggers an emotional response. Because fear was so endemic to the existence of early humans, due to disease, animal attacks, starvation, and natural disasters, the brain eventually found ways of coping with fear. According to Newberg and company, our greatest inventions came about as ways to resolve fears, e.g., tools, weapons, the procedures for banding together for mutual defense. Similarly, laws, culture, and religion were also adaptive strategies.[13] Because humans were so effective in developing responses to dangers, the evolutionary processes brought about a "cognitive imperative," an inner compulsion to analyze reality and develop responses to danger, need, or existential problems. This ability is an adaptive feature of human existence.

The cognitive imperative naturally sought a resolution to the problem of death. According to Newberg and company, the cortex would have engaged the limbic system and the ANS, thereby stimulating an arousal response. Because of the persistence of death in human experience, the cognitive imperative would have stimulated an unceasing search for an

---

11. Newberg et al., *Why God Won't Go Away*, 53.

12. When used by authors in the life sciences, the word *myth* does not have the same meaning as in popular usage, namely, a story or common belief that is false. So I am using the term here in that more neutral manner.

13. Newberg et al., *Why God Won't Go Away*, 60.

answer to death and the questions surrounding it. Myth emerged as the brain's way of resolving the problem through metaphorical stories (e.g., Eve eating the apple, Pandora opening a box).[14] Newberg and colleagues observe that myths employ paired opposites, such as gods/humans, heroes/monsters, heaven/hell, and life/death. The tension is resolved by the actions of the gods or spiritual powers, e.g., how Jesus' dual nature and resurrection from the dead overcome sin and death.[15]

Myths use the same neurological processes involved in our responses to concrete problems.[16] A "causal operator" enables us to find a "cause" of something, as when a person hears a roar and then attributes that to the presence of a lion. A "binary operator" (the part of the brain that forms the polar opposites) enables the mind to analyze reality so that we are able to orient ourselves toward it. Due to fear, the cognitive imperative engages the binary function to make sense of the "metaphysical landscape," by concocting polar opposites (essential in mythmaking). The crucial brain structure in this process is the parietal lobe which contains the neurological structures for the causal and binary operators and also the centers for language (also needed in the generation of myths).[17]

Newberg and his coauthors offer the following scenario to illustrate how mythmaking served an adaptive-survival function. A primitive hunter hears a twig snap and wonders whether it could be due to the presence of a leopard. The right brain calls to mind memories of previously being chased by a leopard, and the left brain surfaces the fear of the previous experience. Rather than verify the actual presence of a leopard, the hunter flees. In this case the (unanswerable) question about a snapping twig leads the hunter to generate a kind of myth. The cognitive imperative leads him to seek an answer by the engagement of his analytic powers. The causal operator gives an explanation and the binary operator frames the problem in terms of polar opposites (leopard/no leopard). With the agreement of the left and right brains, logical ideas are transformed into emotionally felt ideas, thus resolving the uncertainties and giving the hunter a picture of the situation to which he could react.[18] In this case, it is belief that enables

14. Newberg et al., *Why God Won't Go Away*, 61.

15. Newberg et al., *Why God Won't Go Away*, 62.

16. Newberg et al., *Why God Won't Go Away*, 63.

17. Newberg et al., *Why God Won't Go Away*, 65.

18. Newberg et al., *Why God Won't Go Away*, 69.

survival, which is precisely the purpose of the cognitive drive. Such stories are really the underpinnings of religious myths.

Newberg and company then describe how myths about death were generated. A primitive hunter-chieftain sees the dead body of a companion lying on the ground inside their dwelling, where a fire is slowly burning itself out. Questions about the meaning and implications of the death of his fellow hunter go through his mind, causing anxiety and fear. Then

> as the last flames sputter and die, an intuition strikes him: the fire was once bright and alive, but now [is] gone, and soon there will be nothing but lifeless gray ashes. As the last wisps of smoke rise to the heavens he turns to the body of his fallen friend. It occurs to him that his comrade's life and spirit have vanished as completely as the flames. Before he can consciously phrase the thought, he is struck by the images of the very essence of his friend escaping to the heavens, like smoke, the rising spirit of the fire.[19]

He experiences "arousal responses" caused by the frustration and confusion in the left brain (which deals with logic and problem-solving). Interpreting the left brain's "frustration" as fear, the amygdala triggers a limbic fear response that engages the arousal system. At this point, the primitive chieftain-hunter draws an analogy between the dead person and the fire: just as the smoke arises from the dying embers, so the "spirit" of the deceased hunter rises to the sky and settles on the mountain in the form of mist. This analogy is generated by the right brain, whose purpose is to offer intuitive responses. The intellectual idea of the spirit rising (left brain) is matched with a right-brained solution. The agreement of both sides of the brain results in positive neural discharges moving through the limbic system, which stimulates the pleasure centers of the hypothalamus. The activation of the quiescent system allows the chieftain to experience calmness. At one level, brain activity has brought relief from grief and despair, but it has also found a way to "liberate" a person from the power of death. The survival of the spirits of the dead is not just a cognitive idea that is understood, but a reality that is "felt."[20] It is precisely for this reason that myths have enduring power in human cultures. The other members of the chieftain's clan will accept the mythic narrative not so much because they

19. Newberg et al., *Why God Won't Go Away*, 71.
20. Newberg et al., *Why God Won't Go Away*, 71–72.

cognitively accept an objective truth, but rather because they are able to experience its truth through their own "Aha!" moment.[21]

For Newberg and company, the goal of ritual is to enable the self to blend into a larger reality.[22] For most people, however, ritual will only foster a sense of oneness with other people, e.g., fellow worshippers. But that, too, is important: by enabling group cohesion, ritual promotes human survival. Because rituals tend to teach the uniqueness or set-apartness of a group, group cohesion and cooperation are strengthened, thereby leading to better protection from enemies and sharing of food and other resources.[23] Since ritual fosters survival, it necessarily has a biological basis.

According to Newberg and company, rituals usually involve feelings of "tranquility, ecstasy, and awe" that bring about "unitary states" (i.e., spiritual transcendence), and both of these realities have a neurobiological basis. Specifically, the "transcendent unitary states" result from the effects of rhythmic behavior on the hypothalamus and the ANS (and other parts of the brain). Ritual behaviors such prayer, meditation, and participation in a public liturgy lower blood pressure and decrease a person's heart rate and respiration, reducing the levels of the hormone cortisol, which creates positive changes in the functioning of the immune system. Since the ANS regulates all of these functions, ritual clearly has an effect on the ANS and its associated responses. Rhythmic behavior, specifically, alters the autonomic response in the quiescent and arousal systems, e.g., faster rhythms cause more activity within the arousal system, which necessarily makes the hippocampus work harder to establish equilibrium. Because the hippocampus controls the flow of information between different parts of the brain, its calming action in the face of overstimulation deprives some areas of the brain of information (neural input) needed for their functioning. This includes the OAA area—that part of the brain that enables us to distinguish ourselves from other things in our environment and to orient ourselves within our environment. Any deprivation to the OAA—which needs a constant flow of information—can result in it becoming "deafferented," that is, operating with reduced input. This in turn results in "softer boundaries" between the self and the environment, in

---

21. Newberg et al., *Why God Won't Go Away,* 73.

22. As we will see, not all writers focus on the idea that ritual brings about mystical union or a sense of oneness with a corporate body of believers/fellow worshippers.

23. Newberg et al., *Why God Won't Go Away,* 81.

short, a "unitary experience."[24] Specific ritual behaviors that bring about such an effect include meditation and slow chanting.[25]

Repetitive, rhythmic behavior is also associated with strong emotional states. In fact, ritual behavior involving dancing and drumming affect the limbic and autonomic nervous systems, which control emotions. But rhythmic behavior combined with other ritualistic behaviors such as fasting, hyperventilation, and the inhalation of incense can affect brain function so as to cause altered states of awareness. But even profound bows, prostrations, and exaggerated hand and arm movements can lead to altered states. When such actions are noticed by the amygdala, the result is "mild fear" and an arousal response, which if "blended" with a hyper-quiescent state brings about "religious awe."[26]

The experience of awe is heightened when combined with olfactory stimulation because certain smells trigger certain emotions (e.g., lavender brings about calmness, while acidic smells trigger anger and rage). This happens because the amygdala receives olfactory information that leads to the response of watchfulness/alertness.[27] In short, ritual actions heighten the emotions associated with religious experience. Newberg and his coauthors point out, however, that the chemical stimulation of the ANS alone cannot produce the strong emotional states of religiosity; only rhythmic and ritualistic behavior can do that. Additionally, ideas with profound cognitive resonance are needed to produce the full emotional impact of ritual. Thus Newberg and his cohorts conclude that ritual and religious meaning must work together in order to produce an altered state of mind. For example, a person who meditates has to be motivated by a belief in the existence of God and in the possibility of achieving fellowship with God.[28]

What then is the connection between myth and ritual from a bio-evolutionary perspective? Essentially, ritual is a way of bridging the gap between humanity and God. For Newberg and company, brain neurobiology causes experiences that we interpret as encounters with God. The assurances offered by religion (with respect to death, the afterlife, and judgment) are merely ideas, but rituals enable beliefs to be experienced by the body so

24. Newberg et al., *Why God Won't Go Away*, 86–87.

25. Newberg et al., *Why God Won't Go Away*, 87.

26. Newberg et al., *Why God Won't Go Away*, 88.

27. Newberg et al., *Why God Won't Go Away*, 89.

28. Newberg et al., *Why God Won't Go Away*, 90.

that they seem real.[29] Through ceremonial action and bodily experience, the Eucharist, for example, substantiates the biblical story about fellowship with Jesus, enabling us to "feel" what we believe. Thus, ritual is not so much about garnering social benefits (cohesion, respect for authority, lessening of tensions), but rather is a way of "acting out" the myths of religion.

Naturally, the brain has a role in the enactment of myth through ritual, with the controlling of movement and action by the premotor area of the brain being vital. While there is a compulsion to act out our thoughts, the AAA (Attention Association Area of the prefrontal cortex) focuses our attention so that we do not act out all of our thoughts. The existence of this inhibition mechanism proves an inherent need to turn ideas into actions. There was actually an evolutionary basis to this particular impulse: the rehearsal of survival actions such as running, jumping, fighting, stalking, etc. helped our primitive ancestors to hone these necessary survival skills. Because myths address ultimate concerns, they naturally hold our attention, and the compulsion to enact ideas led to our translating myths into bodily movements.

Newberg and company opine that some ancient human ancestor discovered the rhythmic behaviors that created the neurobiological activity that produced feelings of transcendence. The visceral, palpable experience in coordination with symbols and mythic narratives led to the creation of ritual.[30] Ritual persists in human existence because it weds neurobiological function and substantive content. That is, we experience the mythic story and its resolution to life's problems and questions in a way that is transformative. To remain relevant, a ritual has to find a balance between the rhythms that create neurological responses and the mythic content. If the "rhythms" do not generate the proper autonomic and emotional responses, a ritual loses it power; if the symbols and themes become irrelevant, spiritual meaning will decay.[31] The neurobiological basis of ritual also explains its prevalence in human culture: ritual activity is a cross-cultural constant because the unifying states are produced by neurobiological processes. This also explains why (according to Newberg and his cohorts) rituals serve the same purposes across cultures and why rituals remain relevant even in our rationalistic age.[32]

29. Newberg et al., *Why God Won't Go Away,* 91.

30. Newberg et al., *Why God Won't Go Away,* 94.

31. Newberg et al., *Why God Won't Go Away,* 95–96.

32. Newberg et al., *Why God Won't Go Away,* 96.

Finally, while repetitive rhythmic behavior can bring about "unitary states," it is also true that the mind itself can set in motion the neurobiological processes that lead to the unitary states:

> The proper thought theoretically can trigger the mechanism of transcendence but could also push the degree of transcendence to ultimate levels, resulting in profound unitary states, i.e., mystical states. This is what happens when the mind is engaged in the ancient practice of meditation and contemplative prayer.[33]

Besides prayer and meditation, the ritual use of music can also affect brain function, and it is to this matter that we now turn.

Brain Science and Music

Like Newberg and his coauthors, musician and researcher Daniel Levitin relates ritual to the quest for meaning and answers to life's difficult questions. His *The World in Six Songs: How the Musical Brain Created Human Nature*[34] in many ways complements Newberg and company's work.

Levitin notes that music is often part of ritual celebrations that involve memory, e.g., birthdays, anniversaries, and harvest festivals. Religious song is unique because it can only be used at certain times or in certain places. For example, Sir Edward Elgar's "Pomp and Circumstance March (Number 2)" is primarily associated with graduations, and it would be highly inappropriate to play it at sporting events or at weddings. Similarly, the timing of ritual is also important: a doctoral student might think of playing a recorded version of "Pomp and Circumstance" *after* passing his/her examinations, but not *before*.[35] The songs of religious rituals also have a narrower scope of use than mere "seasonal songs" (e.g., "Jingle Bells," "Deck the Halls"). While the latter could be sung throughout the period of late November to late December, singing "Silent Night" apart from Christmas Eve (and possibly the days surrounding December 25) would be highly unconventional.

Levitin observes that music works particularly well in tandem with actions because:

33. Newberg et al., *Why God Won't Go Away*, 97.

34. Levitin, holder of a PhD in neuroscience and a one-time performing/studio musician, also authored *This is Your Brain on Music*, a study of the role of music from the perspectives of neuroscience and evolutionary psychology.

35. Levitin, *World in Six Songs*, 202.

1. It brings together various bodily actions within a single musical act;

2. It inspires and leads the actions by reaching points of emotional tension at the same time as the actions, and then resolves when the actions conclude;

3. It enables participants to perform the rituals accurately because of the synchronization of music and physical action.[36]

Music promotes the orderly performance of movements so that work is efficient. As demonstrated by research, Down syndrome children can better learn to tie their shoes if the movements are set to music. Similarly, the assembling/disassembling of guns or engines by military personnel are more easily learned when set to song. The "rigidity" in the performance (necessary for the efficient coordination of movements) is enhanced by the music because of the precise synchronizing of words and notes. Additionally, Levitin states, music sets the right emotional tone for ritual (whether joyous or somber), helps with the memorization of ideas and the sequence of movements, and enables multiple participants to synchronize their movements.[37]

The quality of the music, too, has an effect on brain activity. In a "call-and-response song," where a line sung by a leader is repeated by a group, there is both predictability and uncertainty: we can anticipate a repetition but we don't know the musical or textual content of that repeated phrase. The element of unpredictability, Levitin notes, causes excitement (i.e., neural arousal), and the rhythmic elements (produced by percussion instruments) can produce trancelike states (as Newberg et al. suggest). According to Levitin,

> When the beat is predictable, neural circuits in the basal ganglia (the habit and motor ritual circuits), as well as regions of the cerebellum that connect to the basal ganglia, can become entrained by the music, with neurons firing synchronously with the beat. This in turn can cause shifts in the brain-wave patterns, easing us into altered states of consciousness that may resemble the onset of sleep, or the netherworld between sleep and wakefulness, or even a drug-like state of heightened concentration coupled with

---

36. Levitin, *World in Six Songs*, 207.

37. Levitin, *World in Six Songs*, 208.

increased relaxation of the muscles and a loss of awareness of time and place.[38]

While music combined with movement can enable a "flow state" (or the "high" experienced by an athlete), even a simple movement such as swaying induces hypnotic states. Levitin contends that the brain waves produced in these respective states are distinct and are not haphazard.[39]

Like Newberg and his coauthors, Levitin affirms that ritual requires both religious content and the rhythmic production of emotions states. Life proceeds on our believing in the unseen and the unverifiable (e.g., that an airplane will take me safely from New York to Los Angeles), and accordingly religion imparts the beliefs and affirmations that keep society going. Music helps us to hold those ideas in our minds by inducing "peak experiences" (i.e., emotional highs) that endure throughout life. If a piece of ritual music induces a trance, every time the music is subsequently played the belief associated with the trancelike state is confirmed, because the music acts as the agent of this reconfirmation.[40]

The reason that music reinforces belief is that it serves as an effective mnemonic device. Music contains "embedded cues" of melody and rhythm, which are constrained by the form and the style of the music. These are encoded by "a series of statistical maps" and "statistical inferences."[41] This means that the brain does not need to learn every note of a melody or every single chord in a harmonic progression of a particular song, but instead "learns" the basic rules of music. Any "violation" of the rules is remembered as an exception. Thus we "guess" where a song is going based the knowledge of our culture's music. Accordingly, music serves as an *efficient* system for transmitting information and helping it to remain in the memory. For this reason, music is inherently part of religious ritual and belief.[42] Our enjoyment of music today, then, is a product of evolutionary adaptation: our primitive ancestors who made good use of music were able to survive and thrive, and so music became an important part of who we are. Songs associated with rituals "remind us during the life-cycle events that we are part of

---

38. Levitin, *World in Six Songs*, 214.

39. Levitin, *World in Six Songs*, 214.

40. Levitin, *World in Six Songs*, 222.

41. Levitin, *World in Six Songs*, 224

42. Levitin, *World in Six Songs*, 224.

a chain of continuing ceremonies and rituals, participating as our ancestors did, binding our collective past to our personal future."[43]

According to Levitin, music ultimately played a role in the development of human nature. Music motivates the repetitive action that evokes religious beliefs, and the latter in turn enable us to resolve the ultimate, metaphysical questions of life. This resolution helps us to avoid obsessing about problems. In tandem with religion and rituals, music helps us to gain a sense of security and safety that allows us to function, specifically, by enabling us to express repressed emotions, find closure, and "move on with resolve and determination."[44]

Ethology

In his *Ritual: A Short Introduction*, Barry Stephenson explains ritual by drawing on the insights of ethology, the study of animal behavior. According to Stephenson, ethologists view ritual as a point of contact between animal and human behavior. For ethologists, animal "rituals" fall into two categories: (1) instrumental behaviors that alter an animal's environment, e.g., building a nest; and (2) communicative behaviors that send messages, e.g., "dances" that suggest readiness for mating.[45] But in some instances, instrumental behavior is transformed into communicative behavior, a phenomenon known as "ritualization." Specifically, this involves a selective process whereby information and emotional states that ultimately serve adaptive and survival purposes are communicated. Ritualized behavior is functional because it allows for better communication in difficult situations like mating, feeding, controlling territory, and establishing hierarchies and social bonds.[46] Ritualization was inherited from our earliest ancestors because some social behaviors appear to be biologically driven.

One such behavior is ritualized combat, which is essentially the use of nonlethal behaviors and actions to settle disputes with neighbors or fellow tribesmen. It is typified by contests of skill and public insults and mockery that serve to diffuse tensions. These contests and exchanges will end with a festive meal that reconciles opposing parties and focuses attention away from the original dispute. In this respect, ritual combat in human society

43. Levitin, *World in Six Songs*, 224.
44. Levitin, *World in Six Songs*, 228.
45. Stephenson, *Ritual*, 8.
46. Stephenson, *Ritual*, 10.

resembles interspecies combat in the animal world that likewise minimizes mutual harm and thus promotes survival and cooperation.[47] Ritual combat also involves an element of "social control" because it attenuates aggression and therefore lessens the possibility of wanton destruction. But, as Stephenson points out, ritual can also encourage war by removing sympathy and susceptibility to appeasement gestures.[48]

Stephenson cautions us, however, about seeing a substantive connection between human and animal ritual, since it would be impossible to trace rituals back through millions of years of evolutionary history. We cannot say that any human ritual behavior relates directly to an animal behavior.[49] Yet neither is Stephenson willing to say that ritual behavior is solely a product of culture, since ethology posits that we are products of both nature and culture. He argues that there is an "innate body intelligence" involved in ritual behavior, not just cognitive processes such as reflection, weighing of options, and decision-making.

Not surprisingly, Stephenson resists the idea that ritual is solely a cultural development—as if human culture "evolved" and then started engaging in ritual. "Rather, ritualization played an adaptive role in the course of both biological and cultural evolution."[50] For this reason, theories about culture have usually tried to account for the role of ritual in the development of culture. With the great evolutionary advancement of the upper Paleolithic period (ca. 36,000 to 10,000 BCE), came the development of distinctively human behaviors like language, symbolism, abstraction, art, and music. Cave art (such as at Chauvet, France), therefore, does not merely have a decorative purpose but a religious one—perhaps even maintaining a link to shamanistic trances.[51] Stephenson posits that if cave art is a practice of shamanism, then shamanism is likely the "original religious/spiritual expression of humanity," and that caves are the original loci of ritualized acts.[52] Artistic representation, he says, is associated with cognitive development and the ability to experience altered states of

---

47. Stephenson, *Ritual*, 14.

48. Stephenson, *Ritual*, 16.

49. Stephenson, *Ritual*, 20.

50. Stephenson, *Ritual*, 21.

51. "Shamanism" refers to practices associated with hunting, healing, the passage of the dead to the underworld, and the belief that spirits inhabit objects in the natural world such as rocks and trees.

52. Stephenson, *Ritual*, 25.

consciousness (and express these through art). Ritual became the means of representing the "parallel realities" that resulted from increased cognitive development and artistic expressions.

Thus, caves served as sacred spaces that shared knowledge of both the physical and metaphysical worlds. Ultimately, shamanistic ritual practices and spaces served the needs of hunting societies by giving hunters a sense of power in the face of their difficult work. From the questions and concerns associated with hunting grew the myths that are the basis of ancient Greek and Near Eastern cultures, i.e., stories about quests and journeys. Thus, ritual deals with the "gap" between the reality of one's situation and what one hopes for, and in the case of primitive people, the principal hope was for food.[53]

Cultural Anthropology[54]

Traditionally, cultural anthropologists have focused on the role of ritual in transformation, specifically, in expressing and facilitating the various transitions that punctuate human existence: birth, illness, puberty, and death/mourning. The rites that help people navigate these transitions are known as "rites of passage," and these involve three distinct phases:

1. Separation—a person is identified by the community as someone going through a transitional stage of life and is grouped with others experiencing that same transition;

2. Transition—the initiates receive intentional training in the values and habits of the new status (e.g., adulthood);

3. Incorporation—with the transition (or "liminal") stage completed, those entering the new life stage (sometimes called "neophytes") are reintroduced into the society as full members of the community with the rights, privileges, and responsibilities pertaining to the new status position.

A pioneer in the study of the rites of passage was the anthropologist Arnold van Gennep (1873–1957), who compared rites of passage to taking a journey with its phases of leave-taking, transiting, and arriving.[55]

53. Stephenson, *Ritual*, 25–26.

54. This section is based on material from Truscott, *Sacraments*, 69–72.

55. We might note that in previous times, the word *passage* meant a journey, as when

According to van Gennep, each of these phases can involve rites for separation, transition, and incorporation. The purpose of the rites of passages is to mitigate any harm to individuals and to society that might result from the anxiety and sense of loss that comes with transitions.[56] Significantly, he likens the passage to a new status or to a new group as a journey that involves passing through "neutral territory."[57] In initiation, the period of the novitiate has both negative and positive aspects, the former taking the form of prohibitions and restrictions (i.e., "taboos") intended to mentally and physically weaken the novice so that he or she forgets the past life.[58] The positive aspects of rites of passage include instruction in the society's laws and customs, participation in religious ceremonies, and the recitation of religious stories.[59] Van Gennep interprets these experiences mostly in terms of "death and resurrection," with the novice being put to "death" through harsh treatments (beatings, seclusion, intoxication), in order that he or she be "resurrected" (transformed) to the new way of living that is the goal of the transition.

The Romanian historian of religion Mircea Eliade (1907–1986) understood rites of passage primarily in terms of death and rebirth, e.g., the "death of childhood" and one's "rebirth" into adulthood. He drew attention to the "ordeals" of the transitional phase, such as fasting, knocking out of teeth, and circumcision, and how the rites of this phase "reactualized" a community's myths, i.e., recapitulated them in a way that enabled novices to experience their power and significance in the present.[60] These ordeals signify a ritual death that is followed by a resurrection or new birth.[61] This death essentially provides a "clean slate" on which is written the community's sacred history, and the result is the formation of a new person. Thus, the ordeals serve the purpose of preparing one to assume new (adult) responsibilities in the society. Because the rites of initiation have been received from the ancient ancestors, these rites revitalize the community in the very act of reactualizing the ancient myth(s).[62]

---

one "booked passage" on an ocean liner from one continent to another.

56. Van Gennep, *Rites of Passage*, 11–13.

57. Van Gennep, *Rites of Passage*, 15–19

58. Van Gennep, *Rites of Passage*, 8–9, 75.

59. Van Gennep, *Rites of Passage*, 75.

60. Eliade, *Rites and Symbols*, 13.

61. Eliade, *Rites and Symbols*, xii.

62. Eliade, *Rites and Symbols*, 4.

The British anthropologist Victor Turner (1920–1983) devoted much of his work to describing and interpreting the transitional or "liminal" (Latin, *limen* or "threshold") phase of the rites of passage. During this phase, the person to be initiated is "neither here nor there [but] betwixt and between all fixed points of classification, [and] passes through a symbolic domain that has few or none of the attributes of his past or coming states."[63] The initiate, having been stripped of all attributes of his [sic] previous social position, is set apart from the rest of society and secluded in a lodge or camp where he is reduced to an equal status with his fellow initiates. Under the tutelage of community elders, the initiates ponder the ultimate issues facing society, and consider how past generations responded to these questions.

The liminal phase of initiation, according to Turner, is characterized by *communitas*, the temporary suspension of the normal social distinctions and the realization of egalitarian cooperation.[64] *Communitas* is vital for society as a whole because it promotes togetherness over and against the separation of people into social "cells." In "revivalistic" Protestant groups, Turner says, *communitas* tends to restore the social bonds of adherents to what was experienced at a movement's inception. The value of *communitas* is that it revitalizes both the initiates and the entire society.[65] Although no society can function without it, *communitas* carries with it the danger of being exaggerated in religions and societies, such that there is "despotism, over-bureaucratization or other modes of structural rigidification."[66] Ultimately, *communitas* itself requires structure if the physical and material needs of a (religious) movement are to be met—but too much structure could lead to a longing for *communitas*.

Performance Theory

Performance theory provides us with another lens for looking at ritual and its place in the church. Having emerged in the 1980s out of the work of British philosopher J. L. Austin (1911–1960), this approach enables a deep appreciation for the transformative power of ritual. Central to Austin's thought, according to Barry Stephenson, is the observation that "through language, we not only communicate information and develop

63. Turner, "Passages, Margins and Poverty," 393.

64. Turner, *Ritual Process*, 96.

65. Turner, *Ritual Process*, 29.

66. Turner, *Ritual Process*, 29.

propositions about the world—we actually accomplish things."[67] For example, the person who says "I promise to give this gift to your brother," is not merely *describing* something, but is *doing* something, namely, engaging in the act of making a promise. Austin refers to such an utterance as a "speech act."[68] Austin's notion of the speech act is a vital contribution to ritual studies because it overcomes any opposition between saying and doing. Thus, a ritual is not merely "empty words" as is sometimes alleged, but the bringing about of a new reality. The nuptial formula "I now pronounce you husband and wife" does not merely declare a reality, but actualizes it then and there.

At its heart, performance theory is about the relationship between the body and knowing. Ritual has to do with knowing the world and it is precisely through the use of the body that we come to "know." Performance theory sees a relationship between ritual and other "domains" such as play, theater, sports, politics, and tourism.[69] Stephenson notes that ritual has certain affinities with "performance," namely, movement, masking, costuming, and make-up. One instance of this correspondence is seen in the adoption of theater architecture by evangelical churches for their liturgical spaces.[70] Stephenson contends that when at its best, ritual will have qualities of entertainment and efficacy (i.e., is able to achieve an effect). Accordingly, if a ritual is overly prescriptive, it will become too much like work and thus joyless. But at the same time, if a ritual lacks substance and therefore any "transformative power," it will die.[71]

Embodiment is key to performance theory's interpretation of ritual. The way that values and ideas are appropriated is precisely by means of ritual practice which necessarily involves the body. Through ritual the body comes to understand the world, and gain a particular perspective on it. But, in Stephenson's view, embodiment has to do with more than simply making people "susceptible" to the dominant ideas and values of a society or group. We act our ways into thinking and being, rather think our way into new ways of acting. While the Cartesian dictum *cogito ergo sum* ("I think, therefore I am") would privilege reason and cognition over the body and lead to a deprecation of ritual as irrational and opposed to knowledge,

---

67. Stephenson, *Ritual*, 86.

68. Stephenson, *Ritual*, 86.

69. Stephenson, *Ritual*, 87.

70. See Kilde, *When Church Became Theatre*.

71. Stephenson, *Ritual*, 93.

ritual activity with the body is actually a way of knowing. On this point, Stephenson gives the example of pilgrimage,[72] which is a way of gaining knowledge of the sacred. Significantly, a pilgrimage has to be performed, otherwise there is no ritual (and no knowledge). Thus, knowledge is acquired precisely through the actions of the body.[73]

On a practical level, performance theory would lead us to ask whether rites of initiation are about more than symbolizing or declaring ideas. Stephenson suggests, for example, that dancing and drumming for extended periods during initiatory rites might produce altered perceptions of the world, such that participants do not merely gain a new status (as with van Gennep), but effectively accomplish a break from the old self.[74] Ideas and attitudes, he says, come through the ritual actions. Going further, we could say that if there is an action associated with a feeling, then the performance of the action will generate the feeling—in both the "doer" and the "receiver" of that ritual action. Thus, ideas are not simply "absorbed" through the consciousness "but formed, [and] given body through enactment."[75]

Drawing on Talal Asad's notion of ritual as a "technology" for producing a "virtuous self," theologian Nathan D. Mitchell highlights the relationship between ritual and the body in Western monastic asceticism. Mitchel notes Asad's observation that the monastic liturgical life was not understood as the enactment of symbols separate from other monastic activities, but was essential to the monk's acquiring of Christian virtues.[76] According to Mitchell all of the monastic activities prescribed by the Rule of Benedict[77] were aimed at the development of "moral dispositions" and "spiritual aptitudes" that ultimately served God. Mitchell writes

> Ritual is . . . perceived as bodily inscription, as embodied practice, rehearsal, routine. It is a way of acting equally applicable to work in the garden, to a business trip outside the monastic enclosure, or to chanting psalms in the oratory. Obviously, such

72. A pilgrimage is a journey to a holy site associated with divine activity, often involving a saint or other holy person.

73. Stephenson, *Ritual*, 96.

74. Stephenson, *Ritual*, 101.

75. Stephenson, *Ritual*, 101.

76. Mitchell, *Liturgy and the Social Sciences*, 72.

77. The Rule of Benedict, dating from the year 516 CE, is a book of regulatory principles meant to guide the communal life of monks living together under the spiritual leadership of an abbot. Its author, Benedict of Nursia (480–550 CE), founded twelve religious communities in Italy.

an understanding of ritual has nothing to do with ceremonial grandeur, solemnity or "canonicity."[78]

The development of spiritual virtues in this case is achieved through material rather than cognitive means.

The goal of monastic ritual, then, is the creation of a new self through time and struggle. For the monk, there is great pain involved because of fasting, vigils, and the denial of sexual urges. As a "rewriting of personal histories" ritual poses a certain amount of danger because it leads to a discovery of our deepest thoughts and desires. The assumption behind monastic asceticism is that all humans are radically self-deceived and "addicted" to false selves—we want to ignore or downplay the truth about ourselves and our weaknesses. Ritual (especially confession) seeks to counter self-deception and spiritual forgetfulness, by "keeping the fear of God before our eyes and revealing the exact nature of our thoughts to God and to another human being."[79] In replacing rituals of denial with rituals of remembrance, the Rule of Benedict aims for the recovery of one's true human identity through a process involving both mind and body.[80]

Mitchell makes six critical observations about the Rule of Benedict, and the three most central of these could be summarized as follows:

1. Ritual generates thought, rather than the other way around;

2. The body is where God's power and presence is manifested and displayed;

3. The doing and the meaning of a ritual are identical, i.e., the ritual process equals the content.[81]

Mitchell notes that the Rule of Benedict involves a qualitatively different kind of ritual than those studied by previous anthropological researchers (e.g., van Gennep) because: (1) what is ritualized in the Rule is not universal, cross-cultural patterns found in all societies, but rather historically specific emotional experiences; (2) Western monastic ritual has nothing to do with "rites of passage," initiation, or life crises, but is a way of learning to embody Christian virtue; and (3) ascetic ritual is

78. Mitchell, *Liturgy and the Social Sciences*, 72.

79. Mitchell, *Liturgy and the Social Sciences*, 76.

80. Mitchell, *Liturgy and the Social Sciences*, 77.

81. Mitchell, *Liturgy and the Social Sciences*, 77–78.

not about reinforcing the structures of hierarchy, but rather is meant to discipline the self.[82]

Reflections

Newberg and company's work on brain science and religious experience offers an explanation for the role of ritual in producing the emotions connected with religious experience. If the religious emotions and experiences produced by ritual draw participants into closer fellowship with God, then we could say that both ritual and the body are vehicles for encountering God. Accordingly, brain science affirms that God is at work deep in our flesh to reveal himself to us and to enable our response to that revelation. In a way, brain science as applied to religious experience affirms the goodness of the human body as a creation of God, and that God is not ashamed to use the human body for God's own purposes. Consequently, we must reject the neo-Gnostic beliefs that (1) we must escape from the body in order to experience fellowship with God, and (2) the body is of no importance when it comes to religion.

But if brain science calls into question theologies that deprecate the body, our theology would call into question any superficial equation of brain-generated experience with "God." On the basis of Newberg and his coauthors, we cannot conclude that any and all "feelings" and "experiences" are necessarily authentic and are from or of God. Just because a song makes us "feel" a certain way does not mean that it forms a true image of God in our minds or leads us to authentic worship of God. True worship depends on knowing the true God. After all, the Bible witnesses to the human desire to worship what is *not* God, including ourselves and things of our own creation. Hence, the First Commandment is to worship the one and only God (Exod 34:14). Religious experience has to be normed and guided by theology to ensure its authenticity and soundness. When it comes to ritual, theological content in the form of accompanying words and teaching are needed so that rituals can be true to our deepest beliefs.

We need only look to liturgical history for an example of how ritual can be part of the *malformation* of Christian people. The grand architecture, rising clouds of incense, foreign words, and lavish vestments of the medieval Mass may have created a "holy" spectacle that produced a deep, visceral impact on worshippers, but it also denied the gift character of the

82. Mitchell, *Liturgy and the Social Sciences*, 78–80.

Lord's Supper, exalted human effort at the expense of divine grace, and fueled controversy and division.

Certainly, Christian liturgists need to consider the relationship between ritual and the brain and work out the implications of this relationship, for example, by planning worship that appeals to all the senses. In the case of music, they need to ask the aesthetic question about whether a particular song has any "power" to stir the emotions—so that the ideas presented therein might impact the singer's faith. But at the same time worship planners need to consider whether ritual actions, symbols, and music point to the gospel of Jesus crucified and risen from the dead. A ritual experience that stimulates the brain must also stimulate a faith that will sustain a person through doubts, struggles, and the fear of death. Thus, our dictum might be: *only rituals that are deeply rooted in the gospel and serve faith have validity and authenticity for the Christian people.*

The key insight from Levitin's exploration of brain science and music is that music forms memory. As people who are simultaneously saints and sinners, we need God's Word deeply impressed on our hearts and minds. The "sinner" needs to hear God's judgment, while the would-be saint needs to hear the comforting gospel of the forgiveness of sins. But individual confession and forgiveness is not always available, and for many Christians it is never available. Fortunately, a biblically grounded body of songs can stamp God's Word on our memories, and we can "retrieve" the messages that will speak to our needs. If our consciences are plagued by the memory of our sins, a few remembered lines from a song of about God's mercy and forgiveness ("There's a Wideness in God's Mercy") can comfort us. When there is no support system around us, it might be that only those songs that resound in our heads will sustain us.

Over the years, imprisoned and persecuted Christians have found comfort in songs (cf. Acts 16:25), and Christians nearing death have experienced peace through songs that speak of heaven, eternal life, and God's presence even in death ("My Faith Looks Up to Thee," "Precious Lord, Take My Hand"). The positive emotional experience of the persecuted and dying brought about by song is not just due to wishful thinking or the delusions generated by harsh, difficult circumstances. Rather, it is due to the fact that remembered songs express the beliefs that bring peace to sorrowful bodies and minds. Because it generates the brain functions that foster positive, transformative emotions, singing serves as a form of pastoral care that prepares us for death. Like Newberg and company, Levitin emphasizes the importance of ritual content and belief in that content. Thus, it is not just a pleasing tune that comforts the dying, but the belief that God is with the dying person as articulated by the song. In sum, Levitin's exploration of brain function and singing reveals that, far more than just a decorative element in the ritual context, singing transforms the ritual participants. At the same time his work challenges Christian worship leaders to attend not only to musical aesthetics but also to theology and spirituality.

Some readers might think that an exploration of ethology (animal behavior) runs counter to our goal of offering an apologetic for ritual. If "ritual" is something that we share in common with animals, then surely it represents a "lower," more primitive part of us that needs to be transcended, especially if we fancy ourselves as "spiritual." But if what ethologists posit about human ritual and its connection to animal behavior is true, then there is benefit for those who consider themselves "spiritual." As noted above, the link with animal ritual has to do with behaviors that mitigate tension and hostility—what we would today call "peacemaking." Ethology, then, suggests that ritual has had a positive role in human existence, specifically, in preserving human community and creation, which in Christian thinking is the basic intent of God's law. Far from alienating us from God and God's intentions for human community, ritual can help us to fulfill those intentions. Thus, ritual is deeply spiritual.

Van Gennep's work on the "stages" of initiation has practical relevance today, particularly for those churches seeking to recover the ancient baptismal catechumenate. If initiation is a ritual process of journeying from one place to another, then the journey cannot be rushed; a convert must be given time to transit out of the old life and to understand and accept the new life. Converts to Christianity need time to "count the cost" of discipleship (Luke 14:25–33).

Yet many Christian leaders are tempted to baptize individuals as soon as possible after their "conversion experience." While that experience may reflect genuine belief, we might question whether it can sustain the convert through the challenges of Christian life, e.g., responding to critical questions about the Christian faith posed by family members, friends, and adherents of the "old" religion. Jesus in fact warns that not all persons who experience an initial surge of faith is able to endure (Mark 4:5–6, 6–17). While it is true that faith is a gift from God, it is also true that faith comes through means, including instruction based on and steeped in the Word of God. Hence, pastoral wisdom dictates that

Christian initiation should involve instruction that enables a mature faith capable of weathering the storms of life.

It was precisely in order to be pastorally responsible that the Roman Catholic Church revived the ancient baptismal catechumenate and why, more recently, some Protestants have developed their own versions of the catechumenate. Through a staged process of instruction, mentoring, and liturgical participation, the catechumenate helps seekers and converts to make the difficult journey from unbelief (or wrong belief) to faith, from life centered on the self, to life centered on Christ, and ultimately from death to life. Churches without a catechumenate might consider adopting it—or at least begin to think in terms of an initiation *process*.

Victor Turner's observations about the liminal state of initiation seem to accord with the performance theory dictum that "doing is knowing," i.e., that the very act of performing is "knowledge." By being grouped together with others to share in the journey toward a new social status, the initiate does not simply learn *about* the need to treat others as equals, but actually lives out that very equality. Even apart from initiation we can see how participation in liminal experience shapes us toward egalitarianism. The Lord's Supper, for instance, is a kind of liminal experience in that it ritualizes our journey to the future fulfillment of God's redemptive reign, giving us a "foretaste of the feast to come." The very act of gathering around the Lord's Table forms us into a pilgrim people. By receiving the same food, in the same amount, and hearing the same words of promise ("The body of Christ, given for you. The blood of Christ, shed for you.") we recognize our common lot as redeemed sinners who share in the hope of eternal life, even as our pilgrimage on earth continues.

The liminality and *communitas* of the Lord's Supper shape us into people who want to share our vision of God's kingdom with those around us through word and deed. If ritual is capable of transformation via the *communitas* experience, then the Lord's Supper and other rites might be more powerful than we have imagined! Yet because there is always the temptation to reduce the Lord's Supper to the vertical dimension—the forgiveness of *my* sins—catechesis is needed to awaken an awareness of its horizontal dimension, and to inculcate the church's basic beliefs about the Supper so that worshippers can participate intelligently.

Finally, performance theory's insight that we "know" by means of what we do with our bodies may well offer a corrective to traditional Protestant thinking about knowledge attainment. Protestants have tended to focus on communication through speaking and listening, as opposed to seeing, smelling, touching, or moving the body. Moreover, we have tended to deprecate all nonverbal forms of knowledge attainment. Yet over the years, Protestant movements have arisen whose liturgical practices affirm the body.[83] Could it be that performance theory has made explicit what many Protestants have known implicitly for a long time, namely, that religious experience involves the whole self and all its senses? Can we Protestants take seriously the insights described above and thus grow in our appreciation of ritual and how it enables our bodies to experience the truths we proclaim?

Thus far we have discussed ritual only in a broad, general sense. In the following chapter we delve into the specific human behaviors encompassed by ritual, what I call the *components* of ritual.

83. Examples include the Shakers, with their ritual dances, and twentieth-century Pentecost-charismatic worship with its emphasis on extended periods of singing during which participants wave their hands in the air, jump, and dance.

Chapter 3

The Components of Ritual

Introduction

So FAR IN THIS volume, I have sought to define ritual (chapter 1) and then, based on the life sciences, discuss why ritual became part of human experience and how it continues to play a role in human society (chapter 2). In approaching the topic in this manner, I have imitated the method of biblical interpretation used by Martin Luther and his colleagues in Wittenberg, whereby the interpreter seeks to explain a text (or topic) by asking two questions: (1) What is it? and (2) What does it do? The first question aims to define while the second seeks to describe the effects of something.[1] As Reformation historian Timothy Wengert points out, Luther assumed that meaning is gained not just by obtaining the facts about something, but also by discovering its goal and purpose, i.e., its effects on the inquirer.[2]

The purpose of this chapter is to introduce the components of ritual, by which I mean the cultural structures, resources, and materials that are organized into ritual systems. Following the interpretative method described above, this chapter will define each component and then describe its function in Christian liturgy. The assumption is that ritual can only be meaningful for readers when they see the purpose and effects of ritual on themselves and on the church's worship services. While the ritual systems of all religions

1. This is also the approach that Martin Luther takes in his Small Catechism, where he expounds the traditional catechetical components of the Christian faith (viz., the Ten Commandments, Apostles' Creed, Lord's Prayer, baptism, confession and absolution, and the Lord's Supper). With regard to baptism, for example, he first defines the sacrament as "water enclosed in God's command and connected with God's Word" and then describes its effects: "it brings about forgiveness of sins, redeems from death and the devil, and gives eternal life to all who believe it." Small Catechism, *BC*, 359.1–2, 5–6.

2. Wengert, *Word of Life*, 16–17.

involve people, music, space, art, story/myth, movement, and time, the way each of these components is understood and used is unique to the specific religion, and is a reflection of doctrine and beliefs. That is certainly true of Christian ritual. Moreover, as we will see, Christian ritual can even offer a critique of conventional thinking about these ritual components.

People

Rituals require people to enact them and to be acted upon by them. There are two basic categories of ritual in Christianity. First, Christians engage in rituals of *private devotion*, e.g., reading Scriptures, praying, meditating, singing, listening to music, lighting candles, and burning incense. Second, Christians together enact rituals for the *public* or *common services* of Sunday (Word and sacrament), daily prayer, and specific occasions (e.g., marriage, funeral). Our focus in this chapter is the latter category.

Leadership of the liturgical assembly is exercised primarily (but not exclusively) by ordained clergy who are called by God and the church to a public ministry that is centered on the church's liturgy.[3] In speaking the Word of God to the assembly in sermons and homilies, the clergy perform a prophetic role; in presiding at the sacraments and other rituals, they exercise a priestly role, by mediating between the assembly and God. Effectively, clergy "represent" God to the assembly, and the assembly to God. Further, by proclaiming the Word of God in a public liturgy, Christian clergy represent the church to the world, speaking on behalf of the former to the latter.

In a sense, ordained clergy are the church's "ritual experts," having been instructed in the history, theology, and practice of their churches' rituals during seminary studies. In turn they instruct others about the meaning and purpose of rituals, especially baptism and marriage, in order to help them participate fully and actively. Additionally, clergy exercise oversight

---

3. A point of disagreement among Christians is over the nature of the calling of clergy. Protestants do not agree with the Roman Catholic view that ordination confers a sacred (indelible) character on the recipient, such that the clergy constitute a priestly caste as in the Old Testament. Rather, Protestants stress the priestly character of the whole Christian church. Yet Protestants disagree among themselves as to the derivation of ordained ministry. Lutherans would insist that there is a special "office" of ministry for preaching and administering the sacraments that is of *divine* origin. See Augsburg Confession (1530), *BC*, 41 (Art. 5). Other Protestants hold that ordained ministry derives from the priestly ministry of the whole church, and accordingly cannot be considered as anything more than a necessary function within the church.

in ritual matters, e.g., deciding who can or cannot participate in a particular ritual and what kind of behavior or attire is appropriate for participants, and by advising churches on liturgical matters. As leaders and teachers of ritual, clergy are like village elders in traditional societies, who serve as keepers and facilitators of the community's rituals.

Yet Christian clergy do not thereby constitute a higher caste or an elite stratum of the Christian people. Rather, they are *servants* of both God and the local church community, an understanding rooted in the teaching of Jesus (Mark 10:42–45). Accordingly, it is not the mere performance of rituals that gives Christian clergy their authority; rather their authority and legitimacy derive from the spirit with which they enact ritual, namely, one of humility and self-forgetfulness.

The people who gather for Christian public rituals form a "liturgical assembly."[4] Although the earliest Christian worship assemblies were comprised of baptized persons only, these gatherings eventually came to include persons whose participation was limited: those preparing for initiation ("catechumens"), and those undergoing church discipline for serious misdeeds ("penitents").

Catechumens were only permitted to receive communion following their baptism, and penitents only at the time of their public reconciliation to the church. Because participation in the worship assembly requires an understanding of Christian doctrine, liturgical texts (e.g., the creed), and the sacraments, instruction on these matters has long been considered important for baptismal candidates and the newly baptized. In the ancient church prebaptismal spiritual formation lasted up to three years, and this included an intensive period of formation during Lent. This was followed by instruction on the sacraments during the weeks just after baptism, a practice known as *mystagogy* ("teaching on the mysteries").[5] Today Christian worship assemblies generally include members at all levels of knowledge and experience: baptized, committed Christians, those preparing for membership, spiritual seekers, and those who are just plain curious. The challenge for churches with diverse assemblies is to provide for the spiritual

---

4. The term *congregation*, meaning those gathered in a particular place, is less than desirable because it also suggests the entire legal entity of a Christian community, not all of whom may be present for a particular public worship service.

5. The latter half of the twentieth century, in fact, saw a revival of the ancient baptismal catechumenate, with its various rituals, some of which take place during the Sunday worship assembly.

needs of both those well-formed in ritual versus those who lack knowledge and experience in ritual matters.

The Christian worship assembly is more than an audience that gathers for entertainment or enlightenment. Rather, its purpose is to participate in the very life of Jesus Christ and respond with prayer, praise, and thanksgiving. Indeed, the entire assembly enacts the rituals of the church's liturgy; the assembly is not merely acted upon by liturgical leaders. As the Roman Catholic Church's *Constitution on the Sacred Liturgy* (*Sacrosanctum Concilium*) puts it: "In the liturgy the whole public worship is performed by the Mystical Body of Jesus Christ, that is, by the Head *and his members*."[6] The Evangelical Lutheran Church in America's *Use of the Means of Grace* likewise affirms both that "the assembled congregation participates in proclaiming the Word of God with a common voice," and that "the gathered people of God celebrate the sacrament [of Holy Communion]."[7]

The people of the assembly act in reference to God, each other, and the world. The assembly's prayers, acts of self-offering, and songs are directed to God. Yet song is also a means of mutual edification because it implants Christian doctrine and ethics (Eph 5:18–19; Col 3:16). Testimonies, professions of faith (using historic creeds), and gestures of mutual reconciliation (the sharing of the peace) are similarly directed "horizontally" to fellow assembly members for mutual encouragement. Although frequently understood in individualistic terms, the common confession of sins is an act of mutual ministry because it affirms that "I" am not the only sinner present in the assembly. Besides each other, the assembled people minister to the world by expressing their faith in a public service to which the greater community is welcome. In ministering to the world, Christian worshippers fulfill the meaning of the word *liturgy* (Gk., "work for the people").[8]

As ritual actors, assembly members serve a priestly role (cf. 1 Pet 2:9). They offer praise to God on the world's behalf, and bring the needs and concerns of the world and the local community before God in prayer. The assembly, in other words, lives out the "priesthood of all believers," which according to Martin Luther, is the "common ministry" of all Christians who pray for and teach one another—in distinction from the "special ministry"

---

6. *Constitution on the Sacred Liturgy*, 5.

7. *UMG*, Principles 10 and 39.

8. In ancient Greece, the word *leitourgias* was used in reference to actions undertaken for the benefit of the entire community, e.g., serving in a lawmaking body or paying for the construction of a road. Thus, the term is best translated as "work *for* the people," rather than "work *of* the people."

of ordained pastors.[9] While the priesthood of all believers does not mean that "anyone can do anything" in the liturgy at will, it highlights how baptism makes "ministers" of all Christians: a reality that is expressed symbolically in the Sunday liturgy. Hence, laypersons serve alongside the clergy in positions of liturgical leadership, namely, as servers (who assist clergy), readers (of Scriptures and other texts), communion ministers, acolytes (lighters and carriers of candles),[10] and ushers. Frequently, musical leadership is provided by laypersons who serve as choir members, cantors (song leaders), organists, and other instrumentalists, although music programs in large churches are often under the direction of professional church musicians.

Myth/Story

As mentioned previously, people have questions about the deep, transcendent realities of life, such as "Why am I here?" or "What is death?" Myths are the stories that answer these questions. The "Aha!" experience—the moment of deep understanding—generated by a myth leads to the activation of the brain's quiescent system, resulting in a sense of peace and tranquility. Myths have power for a faith community because they enable truth to be part of people's felt experience.

Many Christians, however, are uncomfortable at the mention of "myths" in relation to Christian belief and worship, since in popular thinking a myth is a belief or story that is untrue. For Christians, the divine inspiration of the Bible and its resulting inerrancy rules out any discussion of Christian "myths." Nevertheless, the central narratives of the Christian Scriptures do what myths do—offer solutions to life's ultimate questions. So it would not be possible to discuss ritual from a Christian perspective without a consideration of Christianity's defining stories and how they shape Christian liturgy. But in order to avoid confusion and misunderstanding, I will use the term "sacred story" throughout this section of the present chapter.

Central to the Christian faith is the story of Jesus' death and resurrection, as told in the gospels of the New Testament (Matt 26:14–27:66; Mark 14:1–15:47; Luke 22:14–23:56; John 18:1–19:42). Although each gospel has its own unique details about this story, common to all of them

9. Gritsch and Jenson, *Lutheranism*, 11.

10. For a description of liturgical leadership roles, see, for example, Brugh and Lathrop, *Sunday Assembly*, 75–99.

is the following: Jesus of Nazareth, a Galilean rabbi highly regarded for his teaching, healing, and compassion for marginalized people, is betrayed into the hands of his religious opponents by a member of his own inner circle, is abandoned by the remainder of this group, is denounced by Jerusalem's religious elite, and is condemned to crucifixion by the reluctant Roman procurator of Palestine. After an agonizing physical ordeal on the cross, Jesus dies and his corpse is laid in a borrowed tomb. Three days later, however, he appears to some of his female followers and then to his reassembled inner circle of disciples, whom he commissions to carry on his work of preaching and teaching.

The theological significance of Jesus' death and resurrection is that it atones (makes amends) for human sin and disobedience, such that Jesus is the means for people to be in right relationship with God (John 1:29; Rom 3:25), who would otherwise condemn all humanity to eternal death and separation from him on account of their sin. Essentially, then, Jesus is a substitute for the temple sacrifices of Israel. When people accept the "good news" of Jesus' atoning act through faith, they are saved from God's wrath and final condemnation, since salvation is based on a trusting acceptance of God's promises (Rom 3:21–25). Thus, the Jesus story is good news for those who are troubled by the awareness of their sins and consequently recognize their need for personal redemption from the power of sin and all the demonic powers that afflict humanity.

If the death and resurrection story of Jesus offers freedom from the psychological-spiritual burden of having to face a wrathful God on judgment day, it necessarily "frees" men and women to love their neighbors. Because God's wrath is overcome in the Jesus event, one's life need not be oriented around justifying one's self before others or before God—that is, proving one's worth or rectitude. This is significant, since human brokenness makes the need for self-justification endless. Instead, the believer is now free to serve others, and thus fulfill the law to love one's neighbor as one's self (Lev 19:18; Matt 19:19). Moreover, the person who experiences the love of God through an appropriation of Jesus' self-sacrificial acts desires to likewise give self-sacrificially to others. Accordingly, the Jesus story is foundational for Christian ethics.

Of equal importance to the story of Jesus' death and resurrection is the story of his birth, which is the basis of the doctrine of the incarnation. While all four gospels affirm the humanity of Jesus, two of these (Matthew and Luke) narrate his birth and infancy in order to stress that he was human in all ways. Thus, when Jesus was crucified, there was real human suffering and death—not just the appearance of these. A true human represented humanity on the cross to bear its guilt for them. But with the resurrection, the power of death that affects human flesh is overcome in Jesus (Rom 6:9), such that humanity can now live in the hope of life beyond death. The incarnation serves, then, to assure us that we are redeemed in our totality as flesh-and-blood human beings.[11]

The incarnation is also important because it gives historical grounding to the Jesus story. The Gospel of Matthew locates the birth of Jesus within the sweep of the generations of Israel (1:1–16), and his infancy occurs during the reign of Herod the Great (73–ca. 4 BCE). Luke places Jesus' birth against the backdrop of Roman hegemony in first-century Syria-Palestine with its various rulers (Luke 2:1–3). Similarly, the gospels and the Apostles' Creed indicate that Jesus' ordeal in Jerusalem took place during the governorship of Pontius Pilate (ca. 26–36 CE). Thus, the Jesus story is part of human history, implying that the God of Jesus works *in* the human world, rather than remaining aloof from it. In that sense the Jesus story is not a myth at all, since myths take place in nondescript, quasi-fictional worlds. But neither is the Jesus story mere history that offers good ethical lessons for daily living. Instead, it makes claims about life, death, and eternity that can only be received in faith—believed or disbelieved. The faith element in the Jesus story means that it is more than a "myth" in the traditional sense.

Because of its centrality for faith, the Jesus story shapes the whole ritual complex of the Christian liturgy. Preaching not only tells the story of the resurrection, it is shaped by that narrative in that the preacher seeks to produce a "death and resurrection" in listeners by exposing sin ("killing" them spiritually), and then proclaiming God's forgiveness (making them alive).[12] Preaching itself enacts the Jesus story in the listeners. As for baptism, candidates are plunged into the water as a type of "drowning,"

---

11. Along these lines, ancient Christian authors argued that humanity could not be saved unless God's savior had completely taken on our humanity.

12. In the technical language of the Lutheran Church, this is called "preaching law and gospel," which is based on Galatians 3:23–25 and 2 Timothy 2:15. Although the sixteenth-century Reformers did not bequeath a particular homiletical structure for achieving this dynamic, some Lutheran homileticians have put law and gospel at the center of preaching (see Caemmerer, *Preaching for the Church*; Stuempfle, *Preaching Law and Gospel*), and at least one has proposed a particular structure (see Grimenstein, *Lutheran Primer for Preaching*).

and are then brought out again as a "salvation" from the death of drowning (Rom 6:1–4). The baptismal act not only signifies the "death and resurrection" that is one's conversion or regeneration, but inaugurates a life of dying to sin (repenting) and rising to new life (believing the promise of God's forgiveness). Individual confession and forgiveness (that is, "penance" or "private confession and absolution") serves as a return to one's baptism, in which the confession of sins before a confessor constitutes a "death" that precedes a spiritual "resurrection" accomplished by the confessor's word of forgiveness (absolution).[13] Rituals of healing also enact a passage from death to life: James 5:15, for instance, images healing in terms of being "raised up."[14] Not surprisingly, healing rites often include the baptismal gestures of hand-laying and anointing that "tell us again that we are sealed by the Holy Spirit and marked forever with the cross of Christ, who is health and salvation for the whole world."[15] The ritualizing of death in a funeral service also references the death and resurrection motif by means of two actions: (1) placing a large cloth (the "pall") with an embroidered cross on the deceased person's casket, and (2) situating a lighted paschal candle near the casket to symbolize one's resurrection with Jesus, who himself arose in resurrection light.[16] Finally, the Lord's Supper, like baptism, is a bodily means of participating in the death and resurrection of Jesus. When Christians come to the Lord's Table confessing their sin and brokenness, and then receive the bread and cup that offer participation in the body and blood (Matt 26:26; 1 Cor 10:16b) that save from sin, they again die to sin and rise to a new life. Thus, the church's liturgy not only tells the story of Jesus' death and resurrection through words, but also enacts that story through rituals that require the body's participation.

13. Luther obviously has in mind the image of death and resurrection when he says the following about penance (i.e., individual confession and forgiveness): "What is repentance but an earnest attack on the old creature and entering into a new life?" Large Catechism, *BC*, 466.75. See also *ELW*, "Individual Confession and Forgiveness": "Confessing our sin involves a continuing return to our baptism where our sinful self is drowned and dies; in the gift of forgiveness, God raises us up again and again to new life in Jesus Christ" (243).

14. The Greek translated as "raise up" in James 5:15 (*egerei*) is also used by Luke (Acts 3:15; 4:10) and Paul (Rom 4:24; 1 Cor 15:15) in reference to Jesus' own resurrection. Thus, James connects healing to the Jesus story.

15. *ELW*, 660.

16. *ELW*, 647.

Time

Closely aligned with myth/sacred story is sacred time. The church calendar (or "liturgical calendar") focuses on the central stories of the life of Jesus Christ: his birth, manifestation as the divine Son of God (epiphany or *theophany*), temptation, suffering, death, resurrection, and promise to come again. The yearly cycle of Christian feasts (joyful celebrations) and holy days (solemnities) is a complex of symbolic motifs that expresses the church's understanding of how God is at work in the lives of people now. As liturgical historian Maxwell E. Johnson puts it:

> The liturgical year ... celebrates precisely our baptismal identity in Christ as his people, his body in the world. Christmas [for example] is not about baby Jesus in the manger, "back there and then" but about *our* baptismal birth in the adult Christ *today* as he is born anew in us ... through the Spirit who brings the "glad tidings" of salvation—the one salvation—to us now. Easter and Pentecost are about *our* death and resurrection in Christ *today*, our Passover from death to life in his Passover, through water and the Holy Spirit in baptism. Lent is about *our* annual retreat, our annual re-entry into the catechumenate and order of penitents in order to reflect on, affirm, remember, and reclaim that baptism. Advent is about *our* hope for fulfillment in Christ when "he will come to judge the living and the dead," a hope solidly grounded in the baptismal Spirit-gift who is the very down payment and seal of our redemption.[17]

Thus, Christian sacred time points beyond itself to the ultimate truth about the Christian's life in Jesus Christ in the present, and in so doing, renews faith.

The Christian liturgical calendar actually contains two overlapping cycles: the *temporal cycle* focusing on the feasts and holy days associated with the life of Jesus, and the *sanctoral cycle*, with its commemorations of saints, martyrs, evangelists (compilers of the New Testament gospels), and other distinguished Christians throughout the ages. In distinction to the joyous feasts and festivals, *solemnities* are days of subdued observance dedicated to reflection and fasting (e.g., Ash Wednesday and Good Friday).

Chief among the yearly observances of Christians, and actually the first to emerge historically, was Easter, the day of Jesus' resurrection from the dead (also known as *Pascha*). As early as the second century CE

---

17. Johnson, ed., *Between Memory and Hope*, xii. Emphasis original.

Christians in Asia Minor were celebrating the Lord's death and resurrection. For a while there was disagreement as to whether Easter should be observed on a Sunday, since the Lord's resurrection occurred on that day, or always on the Jewish Passover (14 Nisan in the Jewish calendar), since the New Testament Gospels all connect Jesus' death to that feast (Matt 26:2, 17; Mark 14:1, 12; Luke 22:1, 7; John 13:1). The question was finally resolved in the fourth century with the decision to celebrate Easter always on a Sunday. Over time the Easter-Pascha was elaborated with the observance of the events during the last week of Jesus' life (passion week), as well as his ascension to heaven and the sending of the Holy Spirit forty and fifty days after the resurrection respectively. Lent, a pre-Easter season dedicated to fasting, self-denial, and acts of charity, emerged in the fourth century. Since the reckoning of the date of Easter is tied to the appearance of the first full moon of springtime (in the Northern Hemisphere), the calendar date of Easter varies from year to year.

The first festival of the Christmas cycle to emerge was not the December 25 celebration of Jesus' birth in Bethlehem, but rather the observance of his baptism or *theophany* on January 6, which comes to us from early third-century Egypt. The first sure evidence for an observance of Jesus' birth appears in mid-fourth century Rome. Why Roman Christians at that time began celebrating the Lord's birth is a matter of speculation and theory. According to one theory, Christmas may have been instituted as a reactive countermeasure to a late December Roman sun-god festival; the former was meant to draw Christians away from the revelries associated with the latter. Another hypothesis is that Christmas results from a complex series of calculations that made the days of Jesus' conception and death coincide on March 25,[18] such that his birth would have occurred nine months later on December 25. Yet these theories are not mutually exclusive: Christmas may have been established in reaction to a pagan festival and then justified with the calendrical calculations. Like the Easter-Pascha, Christmas was eventually elaborated with a preparatory season (Advent) and an extension of the celebratory period afterwards up until January 6. Unlike the "movable feasts" of the Easter cycle, the dates of Christmas cycle feasts ("the Nativity of our Lord," "the Epiphany of our Lord") are fixed on December 25 and January 6 respectively.

---

18. March 25 in the old (Julian) calendar was the first day of spring, which corresponded with the Jewish feast of Passover.

Besides annual feasts, Christian ritual time also gives importance to the week through the observance of Sunday as the principal day for public worship services. Although Sunday was probably not universally observed in the apostolic era, it was well established in the second century in many places and became universal by the early third century. It must be stressed that Sunday was never meant to replace the Jewish sabbath as a day of rest, but rather to be a day for public worship services.[19] One of the earliest Christian apologists (defenders of the faith), a Roman citizen named Justin, states that Christians gathered for worship on Sunday not only because it is the day of Jesus' resurrection, but also because Sunday was the first day of Creation.[20] Early Christian sources also indicate that Christians observed Sunday as an expression of preparedness for Jesus' second coming, rather than a commemoration of his resurrection.[21]

Besides Sunday, other days of the week have held importance for Christians. The tradition that Judas's plot to betray Jesus began unfolding on a Wednesday and that Pilate's condemnation of Jesus occurred on a Friday commended these as days for fasting.[22] Each day of the week has been used by Christians for daily prayer and praise, whether individual or communal, following the Jewish custom of praying three times daily, at morning, noon, and night (Ps 55:17). Christian daily prayer evolved into the divine office, the cycle of prayer services held throughout the day. While monastic communities gather for communal prayer as many as six times per day, parish churches and cathedrals generally have only services of morning and evening prayer.

Essentially, the liturgical year, to borrow Asad and Mitchell's phraseology, is a "technology" for enabling the body to become attuned to the central Christian narratives and their meanings. At least in the northern latitudes of the earth, the observance of Christmas in late December juxtaposes the story of Jesus' birth with the concrete experiences of colder temperatures and the gradual lengthening of daylight hours (from the winter solstice onward). The observance of Easter relates Jesus' death and resurrection to warmer temperatures, longer hours of sunlight, and the re-emergence of vegetation into a previously barren landscape. The linking of sacred story and climatic seasons moves the former out of realm of remote history or

19. Bradshaw and Johnson, *Origins of Feasts, Fasts and Seasons*, 13.

20. Justin Martyr, *First Apology*, 67.

21. Bradshaw and Johnson, *Origins of Feasts, Fasts and Seasons*, 13.

22. *Apostolic Constitutions*, VII.23.

mythology and into the world of everyday human experience. Because climatic seasons bring with them changes in air temperatures and levels of sunlight that effect the body, the joy of the birth of Jesus, our True Light, is linked to our joy at the increased hours of sunlight. Seeing and smelling new life in spring is linked with the story of Jesus' rising to new life, such that the former helps us to experience the latter in our bodies. (Since the climatic seasons are reversed in the Southern Hemisphere, Christians there must look for other natural associations between the church year and natural seasons.) The practices of fasting and feasting on certain days further serve to engage the whole person in the liturgical celebration. When these practices enable the body to become *well*-attuned to certain observances, every experience of hunger or food deprivation will remind one of Lent and Jesus' trials during the last week of his life, and every feast will remind one of Easter. Essentially the observance of sacred time by Christians is a way for the sacred stories to indwell the Christian and the Christian to indwell the stories such that faith is evoked and strengthened.

Music

The sacred stories unfolded in the church's liturgical calendar are celebrated and proclaimed in its songs. Christian music and song, of course, owe much to Judaism. Following the practices of the Second Temple liturgy and Jewish private worship, early Christian sacred music was essentially the singing of psalms. Hence, we find the admonition to "sing psalms, hymns, and spiritual songs" (Eph 5:18–19; Col 3:16). Two patterns of psalm use emerged in the ancient church: (1) singing the psalms in numerical order, a practice with origins in fourth-century monasticism, and (2) the singing of those psalms deemed appropriate for specific times, e.g., services of morning and evening prayer. There then arose two cycles of psalms, one specified by the Rule of Benedict (sixth century) and used primarily in monastic churches, and a "secular" cycle used in cathedrals and parish churches, based on ancient Roman liturgical practice. We can identify three manners of psalm recitation:

1. *Antiphonal*, whereby two groups alternate the singing of either whole or half verses using psalm tones (short melodies) with a melodic refrain (antiphon) sung before and after the psalm, and sometimes after

each psalm verse or a group of verses (a method associated with the introit and communion psalms of the mass);

2. *Responsorial,* meaning sung in response to the first Scripture reading of the mass or the Scripture reading of the prayer office, often with a refrain sung by the liturgical assembly;

3. *Direct singing,* that is, the singing of an entire psalm text without a refrain. This approach was used to sing those psalms that replaced the Alleluia of the mass during penitential seasons. During the Reformation, Reformed-Calvinist Christians in Switzerland and Scotland became famous for their collections of *metrical psalms*, i.e., vernacular psalm texts sung to familiar hymn tunes. Two early examples of note are the Genevan (1539) and Scottish (1564) psalters. In England, vernacular psalms were set to a form of chant sung by choirs in four-part harmony ("Anglican Chant"), while metrical psalms were provided for congregational use.

The twentieth century saw a revival of psalm singing, with the development of new tones for chanting the psalms, collections of chanted psalms, and metrical psalters.

But Christian song eventually came to encompass the use of texts other than psalms. Forms typically sung by the entire assembly include hymns and other songs of praise, as well as fixed liturgical texts that express the praise relevant to a particular part of the liturgy (e.g., the Gloria in excelsis at the beginning of the Service, the Sanctus during the Holy Communion). "Contemporary worship" services include an extended segment of praise (thirty minutes or more) at the beginning of the service. In the Pentecostal-charismatic tradition, the assembly may engage in spontaneous "singing in the Spirit," or, if the language is unknown, it may "sing in tongues." In the so-called "liturgical" churches, leaders sing prayers and other texts, sometimes engaging in a sung dialog with the assembly. In Orthodox and Oriental churches just about all texts are sung, resulting in "heightened speech" that gives the service a solemn, otherworldly feeling—which suggests that the worship of the earthly church is joined to that of the heavenly church.

Choirs have played an important role in Christian worship, although that role has changed over the centuries. The rise of the *schola cantorum* ("school of songs") in the ancient church reflects the institutionalization of the church during the Constantinian era. The schola's purpose was to sing the important texts of the mass and provide other ceremonial music. From the patristic period until the Reformation, practically all singing in Christian worship was that of the choir. The Reformers, however, gave renewed impetus to congregational singing, but not at the expense of choirs whose contribution was still deemed necessary. While people today think that the choir's liturgical role is primarily aesthetic—it sings "anthems" (biblical choral pieces) to beautify the service and heighten its solemnity—many churches encourage choirs to lead and support the assembly in its singing.[23] This effectively makes the choir part of the assembly (its "rehearsed" component), rather than distinct from it as in the past.

The emphasis on songs and singing in Christian worship might lead us to wonder why Christians sing in the first place. The most central reasons are the following:

To praise God. Praise in the Bible does three things. First, it extols the person and character of God, e.g., his goodness and greatness, or his role in creation (Ps 8). Second, praise acknowledges and glorifies God's saving deeds for his people, as when Moses and the Israelites celebrate their deliverance from the pursuing Egyptian armies in Exodus 15. Third, praise recounts an individual's deliverance from enemies (Ps 30) and thanks God for it. Gratitude for divine benevolence bestowed on an individual and the community of Israel is expressed in the *Magnificat* or "Song of Mary" in Luke 1:

> Then Mary said:
> My soul magnifies the Lord,
>> and my spirit rejoices in God my Savior!
> For He has looked with favor on the humble state of His servant.
>> From now on all generations will call me blessed.
> For the Mighty One has done great things for me.
>> Holy is His name.
> His mercy extends to those who fear Him,
>> from generation to generation.
> He has performed mighty deeds with His arm;
>> He has scattered those who are proud
>> in the thoughts of their hearts.
> He has brought down rulers from their thrones,
>> but has exalted the humble.
> He has filled the hungry with good things,

23. *UMG*, Principle M-11.

but has sent the rich away empty.
He has helped His servant Israel,
remembering to be merciful,
as He promised to our fathers,
to Abraham and his descendants forever. (vv. 46–55)

In this text, God is gloried for selecting Mary to be the mother of Israel's messiah and for being faithful to Israel by subverting the rich and powerful. The *Magnificat* has traditionally served as the main song of praise ("Gospel Canticle") in the service of Evening Prayer, the ritual logic being that just as Mary watched and waited for the fulfilment of God's Word in her life (i.e., the messiah's birth), so the church watches and waits in the dark of night for the coming of God's messiah.[24]

To lament. While songs of praise express joy and gratitude for God's benevolent actions, songs of lament express sorrow, grief, and outrage at the presence of evil and the absence of God in the midst of evil. Well known to Christians for its use on Good Friday is Psalm 22:

My God, my God,
why have You forsaken me?
Why are You so far from saving me,
so far from my words of groaning?
I cry out by day, O my God,
but You do not answer,
and by night,
but I have no rest.
Yet You are holy,
enthroned on the praises of Israel.
In You our fathers trusted;
they trusted and You delivered them.
They cried out to You and were set free;
they trusted in You and were not disappointed.
But I am a worm and not a man,
scorned by men and despised by the people.
All who see me mock me;
they sneer and shake their heads:

24. Messerli and Pfatteicher, *Manual on the Liturgy*, 284.

"He trusts in the LORD,
    let the LORD deliver him;
let the LORD rescue him,
    since He delights in him." (vv. 1–8)

In a similar vein is Marty Haugen's "O God, Why Are You Silent?," whose second stanza is:

My hope lies bruised and battered,
my wounded heart is torn;
my spirit spent and shattered
by life's relentless storm;
will you not bend to hear me,
my cries from deep within?
Have you no word to cheer me
When night is closing in?[25]

In both the Magnificat and the hymn by Haugen, God's silence brings despair to the speaker, who earnestly asks for a response from God. Through lament, the church gives theological and emotional balance to its winsome, upbeat praise, while injecting an element of reality into its worship.

To instill doctrine. If Christian song can express the emotions of joy, gratitude, and despair, it can also function in a more intellectual, cognitive way by instilling doctrine. One of the earliest known Christian songs, the so-called "kenotic hymn" in Philippians 2, is essentially the doctrine of Christ (Christology) in song. It skillfully compresses the Jesus story into a few lines with concrete images that make the theological ideas memorable, and singing these lines further serves to make them memorable.[26] Songs that confess the person and works of Christ are found in all periods of Christian history, including the hymnody of Ambrose of Milan,[27] Marcus Aurelius Prudentius,[28] Martin Luther,[29] and Charles Wesley.[30] But besides Christology,

---

25. *ELW*, #703.

26. See "Jesus Christ is Lord," *Music Sourcebook for Lent and the Three Days*, S429.

27. See "Savior of the Nations, Come," *ELW*, #263.

28. See "Of the Father's Love Begotten," *ELW*, #295.

29. See "O Lord, We Praise You," *ELW*, #499.

30. See "Hark! The Herald Angels Sing," *ELW*, #270.

the doctrines of the Trinity,[31] the Holy Spirit,[32] atonement,[33] and eschatology[34] are also frequently treated in hymns.

Similar in function to hymns and songs that reinforce central doctrines are those that expound the theology of the sacraments. As the Evangelical Lutheran Church in America puts it: "Music surrounds and serves the celebration of the sacraments. As part of God's creation renewed in Christ, the people of God sing around the elements, words, and actions that bear God's grace."[35] Through song, assembly members teach each other about the gifts imparted in baptism and the Lord's Supper, thereby sharing in the catechetical work of pastors and lay professional teachers. Two contemporary examples of sacramental songs are Ruth Duck's "Wash, O God, Our Sons and Daughters,"[36]and Delores Dufner's "What Feast of Love."[37]

To share the gospel. Many Christian hymns and songs share a message of good news to those seeking salvation and/or offer comfort to those with troubled and doubting consciences. Like doctrinal songs, evangelistic songs narrate the Christian story, but do so by expressing it in a "for you" way in order to evoke personal faith. One of Luther's earliest hymns, "Dear Christians One and All Rejoice" (1523), tells the salvation story as it speaks gospel promises directly to troubled sinners. ("The foe will shed my precious blood; all this I suffer for your good; my life o'er death will triumph").[38] More than a statement of an abstract truth, "Dear Christians" shares the gospel in a very personal way, becoming not just a statement of the gospel but a performative proclamation of it.[39]

With a tendency to speak from the perspective of the singer (as opposed to that of Christ), songs from the American gospel hymn tradition likewise expound the story of salvation with the goal of kindling faith. Charlotte Elliot's "Just as I Am"[40] and Fanny Crosby's "Jesus Keep Me Near

31. See "Holy, Holy, Holy, Lord God Almighty," *ELW*, #413.

32. See "Come, Holy Ghost, Lord and God," *ELW*, #395.

33. See "Dear Christians, One and All, Rejoice," *ELW*, #595, stanza 6.

34. See "Lo! He Comes with Clouds Descending," *ELW*, #435.

35. *PW*, Principle M-8.

36. *ELW*, #445.

37. *ELW*, #487.

38. "Dear Christians," *ELW*, #594, stanza 6.

39. On the matter of singing as a performative act, see Kubicki, *Liturgical Music as Ritual Symbol.*

40. *Hymns of Praise*, #343.

the Cross"[41] narrate a personal story of salvation, telling what Christ did for the speaker, suggesting that saving mercy is available to others. In the African American gospel tradition, the experiences of slavery are reflected in songs that share a desire to be free from oppression and to reach a promised land, e.g., "When Israel Was in Egypt's Land."[42]

To form the church for ethics and mission. While the church's life is centered on its Sunday liturgy, it nevertheless has a mandate to take the gospel to the world (Matt 28:18–20). In addition, the faith that is formed in each Christian by the liturgy works itself out in daily human interactions that reflect the love and mercy of Jesus Christ (Gal 5:6; Jas 2:26). In sum, worship leads to mission and service in the world. As *Use of the Means of Grace* puts it:

> In every celebration of the means of grace, God acts to show forth both the need of the world and the truth of the gospel. In every gathering of Christians around the proclaimed Word and the holy sacraments, God acts to empower the Church for mission. Jesus Christ, who is God's living bread come down from heaven, has given his flesh to be the life of the world. This very flesh, given for the life of all, is encountered in the Word and sacraments. [43]

The challenge is to keep this relationship between liturgy and the world before the people of God. According to *Use of the Means of Grace*, assembly song is vital in this regard:

> The assembly is gathered and sent out in song, bearing the witness of Christ to each other and all they encounter. Through music, the Holy Spirit empowers the assembly to participate in God's mission to the world.[44]

> Music bears the biblical word of justice and mercy.[45]

In other words, Christian ritual song forms assemblies in mission and ethics, and songs that do this particularly well can be grouped into six categories:

---

41. *Hymns of Praise*, #450.

42. *With One Voice*, #670.

43. *UMG*, Principle 51.

44. *PW*, Principle M-17.

45. *PW*, Principle M-18.

Commitment

- "Take My Life and Let it Be" (UMH #399)
- "Let Us Talents and Tongues Employ" (ELW #674)

Compassion

- "The Church of Christ in Every Age" (UMH #589)

Evangelism

- "O Zion, Haste" (UMH #573)
- "Shine Jesus Shine!" (ELW #671)

Justice and Peace

- "We Come to the Hungry Feast" (ELW #479)
- "Faith of Our Fathers" (UMH #710)

Trust and Guidance (Living Out the Christian Calling)

- "Jesus Calls Us" (UMH #398)
- "Shout to the Lord" (ELW #821)

Witness

- "Will You Come and Follow Me?" (ELW #798)
- "Jesus Shall Reign" (UMH #157)

Through song, the body of the singer becomes attuned to the work of sharing the gospel and performing acts of love for the benefit of the neighbor. Drawing on Asad and Mitchell's concept, we could say that singing is a "technology" for missional and ethical formation.

Thus, singing in Christian worship is about more than experiencing aesthetic pleasure or strong emotions. The assembly does not merely "consume" the offerings of professional musicians for these purposes. Neither is singing in Christian worship a marketing tool for attracting new members. Because song shares a message that invites newcomers to faith, and is a means of mutual ministry within the assembly, it is not the "possession" of church musicians, who display their talents in order to create a fan base. Rather, song belongs to the whole assembly, and musicians are servants of the assembly. In sum, the church's way of using song transcends Western pop culture's tendency to make song a consumer product for mood manipulation and/or background music.

Just as assembly song is not directed to people for purely pragmatic reasons, neither is it directed to God for self-serving purposes. While Christians may rightly believe that their singing pleases God, it would be problematic to think that it makes God more amenable to us and our prayers—as if God were a needy authority figure who required "softening up" through song. God does not "need" our songs; rather, the assembly needs to sing in response God's surprising mercy and to build up each other in the faith. Using song for these purposes will indeed be God-pleasing.

Dance

Music and song naturally give rise to dancing, whether spontaneous or choreographed. Like song, dance is inseparable from religion. Theologian J. G. Davies observes that the gods of ancient religions were thought to have engaged in dance, and human dance was both a way of imitating the gods and narrating their exploits. When dancing, people experience communion with the gods who were pleased by the dancing of their devotees.[46] Dancing, Davies argues, both effected this communion and was its effect, meaning that dance in pre-Christian religion possessed a sacramental character. It is in fact connected to all of the key components of ancient and modern religions: sacrifice, prayer, rites of passage, and funerals.[47] Referencing the work of John Martin, Davies notes the distinction between (1) dancing associated with rituals of tension (which seek to alleviate anxiety, fear, and uncertainties), and (2) dancing associated with rituals of release (which celebrates positive experiences such as military victory, a successful harvest, or the onset of rain).[48]

The Old Testament contains numerous references to dancing, most of which are positive. For example, Miriam led a dance by women following Israel's deliverance from the armies of Pharaoh (Exod 15), and David danced "with all his might before the Lord" as the ark of the covenant was transferred from the house of Obed-edom to Jerusalem (2 Sam 6:14). Various psalms encourage dancing as an expression of joy:

46. Davies, *Liturgical Dance*, 10–13.

47. Davies, *Liturgical Dance*, 14.

48. Davies, *Liturgical Dance*, 18.

Hallelujah!
Sing to the LORD a new song—
    His praise in the assembly of the godly.
Let Israel rejoice in their Maker;
    let the children of Zion rejoice in their King.
Let them praise His name with dancing,
    and make music to Him with tambourine and harp.
For the LORD takes pleasure in His people;
    He adorns the afflicted with salvation.
Let the saints exult in glory;
    let them shout for joy upon their beds. (Ps 149:1–5)

Hallelujah!
Praise God in His sanctuary.
    Praise Him in His mighty heavens.
Praise Him for His mighty acts;
    praise Him for His excellent greatness.
Praise Him with the sound of the horn;
    praise Him with the harp and lyre.
Praise Him with tambourine and dancing;
    praise Him with strings and flute.
Praise Him with clashing cymbals;
    praise Him with resounding cymbals.
Let everything that has breath praise the LORD!
Hallelujah! (Ps 150)

It would seem that dancing was a natural part of the religion of ancient Israel. In the one instance when dancing was condemned, namely by David's wife Michal, there is a hint that divine retribution was eventually visited upon the critic (2 Sam 6:23)!

By contrast, the New Testament has very few references to dancing, and it says nothing about dancing in connection with Christian worship. Jesus himself mentions dancing in a brief teaching (Matt 11:17) and in the parable of the Prodigal Son (Luke 15:25). The dancing of Herodias in the story of John the Baptizer's execution is the only other gospel reference to the action (Matt 14:6). The most that we can say is that dancing was part of the cultural milieu of the New Testament, which neither encouraged nor forbade it in public worship or for personal recreation.

Dance was generally disdained and condemned by theologians and councils during the patristic era of the church (late first to mid-eighth centuries), whether as a form of recreation or an act of Christian worship.[49] Davies opines that this negativity reflects the bad reputation dancing had gained in Roman cultural due to debauchery and excess (e.g., Cicero's view that it was inappropriate among decent people).[50] Additionally, since dancing in pagan religion portrayed the deeds of the gods, some of which were unseemly in Christian eyes, it is hardly surprising that dancing was rejected by early preachers and teachers. Moreover, any support for dancing would have suggested an approval of pagan religion much to the confusion of the Christian faithful.[51]

But Davies notes deeper reasons for early Christianity's rejection of dance. During the patristic era, he contends, Christianity was developing a greater asceticism, and consequently viewed communion with God as a constant battle against the flesh and its desires. Specifically, the monastic ideal of renouncing the self and its desires became the ideal for all Christians. Related to this shift was a general denigration of the body and a tendency to see dancing as little more than evidence of the body's degraded status. This struggle against the body left little room for any kind of spontaneous movement or dancing. Thus, the association with paganism and a growing ambivalence toward the human body led patristic thinkers to eschew dancing.[52]

In the Reformation era, most prominent church leaders and theologians also rejected dancing. Only Luther was willing to allow dancing at weddings, so long as it did not become debauched.[53] Calvin essentially banned dancing from Geneva altogether because he believed that it led to lewdness. According to Davies, continental Calvinists and English Puritans more or less echoed the patristic era's rejection of dancing. While the Puritan Philip Stubbes acknowledged the Old Testament's positive depiction

---

49. Davies, *Liturgical Dance*, 19–21. Although he could write rather negatively about dancing, Ambrose of Milan did in one instance express approval for it. See Senn, *Embodied Liturgy*, 325.

50. Davies, *Liturgical Dance*, 22.

51. Davies, *Liturgical Dance*, 23.

52. Davies, *Liturgical Dance*, 24–25.

53. Luther, *Sermon on the 23rd Chapter of Genesis*. Cited in Davies, *Liturgical Dance*, 29.

of dancing, he did not view this as a warrant for dancing in his own time.[54] Nevertheless, he indicates that he could approve of a purified form of dancing performed for the purpose of glorifying God.[55]

But, as Davies notes, the "balanced" view of the Puritans was superseded by a rejection of dance in the eighteenth and nineteenth centuries. This was fueled in part by the Cartesian emphasis on thinking, which viewed participation in spiritual realities as primarily a matter of the mind, and gave little worth to the physical movement of the body. The rejection of dancing, in fact, came to be viewed as a sign of a society's intellectual and social progress. Thus, while Victorian society could permit dance as a social activity, it was incapable of viewing it in connection with either religion or reasonable thinking.[56]

The rejection of dance by Christian thinkers and authorities, however, is not a reflection of what actually occurred in churches. While ancient theologians and councils condemned dance, there is nevertheless *some* evidence of dancing taking place in churches during the patristic era, e.g., an anonymous letter of the late fourth century that indicates the occurrence of dancing during the commemoration of St. Polyeuctus.[57] Similarly, Christians danced during the commemoration of St. Cyprian in Carthage in the year 360.[58] But for the first millennia of the church's life, there is no evidence of *liturgical dance*, i.e., dance that was incorporated into the church's liturgy.[59]

During the Middle Ages dancing took place in connection with (1) ordinations (when newly ordained priests danced with their mothers after their first mass); (2) church ales (a parish feast held for the purpose of fundraising); and (3) the Feast of Fools, a celebration held on New Year's Day that featured satirical performances by lower clergy who assumed the roles of higher clergy. But these activities were condemned by church authorities, and in the thirteenth century church councils sought to prohibit dancing entirely.

The prevalence of dancing in the Middle Ages—despite attempts to suppress it—is attributable to two factors. First, while monastic asceticism

---

54. Stubbes, *Anatomy of the Abuses*, 166. Cited in Davies, *Liturgical Dance*, 30.

55. Stubbes, *Anatomy of the Abuses*, 165. Cited in Davies, *Liturgical Dance*, 31.

56. Davies, *Liturgical Dance*, 33–35.

57. B. Aube, *Polyeucte dans l'histoire*, 79. Cited in Davies, *Liturgical Dance*, 43.

58. F. van der Meer, *Augustine the Bishop*, 514. Cited in Davies, *Liturgical Dance*, 44.

59. Davies, *Liturgical Dance*, 44–45.

was viewed as the ideal for all Christians in the patristic era, the sharp distinction made between laypeople and clergy in the Middle Ages meant that lay people were held to lower standards than monks, who were striving for spiritual perfection. Accordingly, the prohibition on dancing was not applied to the laity. Second, laypersons gained a greater sense of ownership over church buildings, since they frequently paid for their construction and helped in their upkeep. So laypeople thought that they could do as they pleased in "their" church buildings, which in the Middle Ages were often the only public facilities suitable for dancing by large groups of people.[60]

Dancing, however, was still a part of church life after the Reformation and some new dances were created in the sixteenth and seventeenth centuries, e.g., the Eagle Dance in Spain, and the "Dances of the Six Youth," who represented the Virgin Mary, three angels, and two devils.[61] The two most significant developments of the nineteenth century were the promotion of the idea that church buildings were for worship only and the emergence of Shakers with their distinctive form of dancing in worship. The inspiration for Shaker dances came from various figures in the Old Testament who danced for joy (e.g., Miriam, David), and a number of their songs mention these individuals.[62] For Shakers, dance was an expression of the equality of men and women and was meant to encourage cooperation and the celebration of the various spiritual gifts. Shakers also saw an eschatological dimension to dance insofar as they viewed dancing as their response to the promise of the messianic age and its fulfillment.

For African churches, dancing in worship is essential. This owes to the fact that African culture does not harbor suspicions about the human body. Elochukwu Uzukwu writes that "Africans tune into the rhythm of life in the world bodily; the self in all its complexity is manifest bodily. Life in the world, as a result, explodes in dance . . . ."[63] Consequently, the body is important to communication and dance is a vital way of interacting with others in Africa. Today in African and African-descended churches, dancing is used to express the joy and adoration of the entrance procession as well as the offertory procession.[64] In African American and African Caribbean

---

60. Davies, *Liturgical Dance*, 57.

61. Davies, *Liturgical Dance*, 60–61.

62. Davies, *Liturgical Dance*, 64–68. For a detailed description of Shaker dance, see Daniels, *Dance in Christianity*, 64–69.

63. Uzukwu, *Worship as Body Language*, 322.

64. Uzukwu, *Worship as Body Language*, 273, 295.

churches, spontaneous dancing will occur throughout the service, although classical dance and flag dances have also been introduced.[65]

European and mainline American churches in the twentieth century have seen a revival of dance. This owes to a growing appreciation for the body as a medium of expression[66] and the resulting shift that took place in the understanding of the nature of dance. By and large, modern dance rejects the idea that dancing tells stories and instead favors the view that it serves as an expression of feelings. Dancing does not present ideas or concepts to be grasped with the mind; rather it presents an emotion that is grasped by the eye and the onlooker actually processes this in his/her body. Essentially, bodily movement is communication, and communication is made through the body. Consequently, dance (especially postmodern dance) does not mean or signify something; it means what it is. "It is kinesthetic movement apprehended by the senses only."[67]

Because the focus of modern dance is movement itself, and since dance is generally detached from debauchery, it now has a greater potential for use in the church. Perhaps with the exception of the most conservative circles, dancing is widely accepted by Western society and by Western Christians. Not surprisingly, the twentieth century saw the emergence of the liturgical dance movement, whose purpose is to promote dance as a way of expressing various aspects of worship (prayer, praise, lament, self-offering). According to Thomas A. Kane, there are five types of liturgical dance, all of which are determined by the structural components of the liturgy:

1. Procession dance, which occurs during the entrance of the ministers, the taking of the gospel book into the midst of the assembly (for the reading of the gospel), the presentation of the offerings at the altar-table, and at the closing procession;

2. Proclamation dance, which is performed as the Scripture lessons are read in order to express them in a dramatic, verbal/dramatic way;

3. Prayer dance, which includes (a) *acclamations* or verbal assents to God's Word by the assembly, and (b) *invocations* or prayers of praise and thanksgiving to God (e.g., the Gloria in excelsis and the Lord's Prayer);

65. Sturge, "Black Churches' Worship," 62; Cosen, "Black Churches' Worship," 64.

66. Davies, *Liturgical Dance*, 74.

67. Davies, *Liturgical Dance*, 77.

4. Meditation dance, which invites reflection on the Scripture readings, but could also occur after the conclusion of the service in order to promote reflection on the whole service; and

5. Celebration dance, which is used during the prelude and postlude in order to set the tone for the service (prelude) or to bring it to a close (postlude). This type of dance could involve the entire assembly and thereby mitigate the impression of a dance "performance."[68]

Despite having found these uses, dancing still remains somewhat controversial as an expression of Christian worship. Nevertheless, dancing in the liturgy is acceptable and desirable for the following reasons:

First, dancing affirms the unity of human nature. One of the ongoing struggles in Christianity is the body/mind or body/spirit duality, that is, the tendency to compartmentalize the human person such that the body is viewed as little more than a shell for carrying the "mind" and the "spirit"— the essential "I" of the person. This duality leads to a denigration of the body and consequently to its abuse and neglect, because of the body's perceived inferiority to the mind/soul. To offer worship through the body—through dance—is to offer not just an expression of the spirit's praise, but to offer the whole self to God. Thus, dance affirms the unity of body and spirit.

Second, dancing affirms the sacramental character of Christian worship. "Sacramentality" has to do with how things of this world mediate humanity's ongoing fellowship with God. Created matter can be revelatory of God, and God is not ashamed to use it to communicate with people. Dancing as a human activity involving the body is revelatory of the joy that will be ours in God's eschatological future. In other words, dancing is a sign of the kingdom of God (Luke 6:23), which has already broken into this world in the life, death, and resurrection of Jesus. Dancing has an affinity to the Lord's Supper because it also uses movement and gesture, and is therefore appropriate within the context of the Lord's Supper to signify the assembly's joyful anticipation of the messianic banquet and to evoke that joy in the present.[69]

Third, dancing promotes identification with biblical images. When a gospel narrative is depicted in dance, the movement of the dance enables us to experience in our bodies the emotions of the person depicted. In that sense, then, dancing can make a biblical passage relevant and meaningful

68. Kane, "Dance, Liturgical," 150–51.

69. Davies, *Liturgical Dance*, 124.

to worshippers, and thus help them to take on the characteristics of the person portrayed in dance. Accordingly, a dance that depicts Christ enables us to become more Christlike.[70]

Fourth, dancing fosters greater participation within the assembly. According to Davies, this happens because dancing (1) reduces "shyness and promotes corporateness," (2) pulls people out of isolation, (3) helps people to become something bigger than themselves, (4) gives individuals an active role in the liturgy, (5) expresses the joy of the Eucharist; and (6) enables the assembly to "experience and embody" the joy of the Lord's Supper.[71]

Finally, I offer two points of caution. First, any dance by a trained dancer should be well-integrated into the liturgy. That is, it should be a true and fitting expression of the liturgical act to which it is wedded (e.g., a reading of Scripture or the presentation of the offerings), or be a true and appropriate expression of the themes that are presented in a particular liturgy. Otherwise, dancing might seem to be a "performance" for its own sake. Second, any dancing or guided movement that involves the whole liturgical assembly should be simple enough for non-trained dancers to perform with only minimal instruction. A complicated sequence of movements that befuddles worshippers could leave them discouraged and thinking negatively about the role of dancing in worship. In that case, the goal of fostering participation is undermined. But dancing and movement in worship, if used thoughtfully, can help assembly members to experience the church's praise, prayer, song, and sacraments at a more profound level.

Postures, Gestures, Processions

Dancing is not the only way that the body is used in Christian worship. Over the centuries, Christians have found different postures and gestures helpful for expressing and facilitating worship. Both practical and symbolic, liturgical processions also served the needs of worship assemblies. These three uses of the body are mentioned in the Bible, but the New Testament generally does not prescribe them, although there are a few exceptions (cf. 1 Tim 2:8). Postures, gestures, and processions are subject to custom, tradition, and discretion. Nevertheless, these are important because they express meaning and imprint that meaning on the bodies of the worshippers.

70. Davies, *Liturgical Dance*, 139–40.

71. Davies, *Liturgical Dance*, 145.

Postures

Posture refers to the different positions of the body, whether standing, sitting, kneeling, or prostrating one's self. In utilizing posture, Christian worship is no different from the ceremonies of civic and cultural life.

Standing is the normal posture for Christian worshippers, especially when singing and participating in solemn rituals, such as confessing the creed or receiving a ritual blessing. Following the custom of the ancient Jews (cf. Luke 18:11–13), and early Christians, many Christians today also stand during intercessory prayer. Standing in worship recalls the response of those healed by Jesus (Mark 2:9) or Paul (Acts 14:10), and so symbolizes transformation and new life. It gives expression to and cultivates an inner attitude of joy. Standing also suggests respect and reverence insofar as it is customary for audiences to stand at the arrival of a dignitary, e.g., a judge, or the President of the United States. At a practical level, standing facilitates whole-body actions such as singing by allowing worshippers to breathe more deeply, and in some cases, it can give them a better view of the presiding minister and the liturgical proceedings.

Sitting is the preferred position for listening and meditation. Except for those spaces where chairs or pews are not available, sitting is nearly the universal posture for the assembly during the reading of the Scriptures and preaching.[72] Worshippers are generally seated for silent meditation. Hence, the seated position expresses an attitude of attentiveness to instruction, much like that exhibited by Jesus' friend Mary (Luke 10:39). The association with silence and meditation has also made sitting a preferred position during intercessory prayer in some Protestant churches. We might note that in the ancient world a teacher sat while instructing his students (Matt 5:1) as a sign of his authority, and this association led ancient churches to provide special seating for bishops and other clergy in their liturgical spaces. However, with the use of congregational seating from the Reformation era onward, sitting no longer underscores clerical authority.

Kneeling is the posture of humble reverence in recognition of the divine presence (Ps 95). Following the example of Jesus' anguished prayer on the Mount of Olives (Luke 22:41), worshippers in some traditions kneel during prayer, both during private devotions and during the public liturgy of Word and sacrament. Besides prayer, kneeling is commonly used while receiving

72. However, in the Roman Catholic, Anglican, and Lutheran traditions, worshippers stand during the reading of the gospel lesson, in order to honor the presence of Christ who speaks directly to the assembly through this reading.

liturgical blessings, the communion elements, and the ashes of Ash Wednesday. Some Christians kneel during parts of the eucharistic prayer in the Holy Communion rite. However, in many ancient churches, kneeling was forbidden during the Easter season in order to maintain a spirit of joy and gladness in response to the Lord's resurrection.

Prostration involves a person lying flat on the ground, often times with limbs spread out from the body. It is a sign of utter submission, particularly when one is in the presence of a higher authority. Yet prostration also expresses adoration or pure worship. Abraham fell face down to the ground when God promised to make a covenant with him (Gen 17:3). One of the ten lepers healed by Jesus returns and throws himself at Jesus' feet, i.e , prostrates himself (Luke 17:16). It was traditional for ordinands to prostrate themselves before the altar as a sign of their submission to God and ecclesiastical superiors. But today this posture is rarely used, especially in Protestantism.

Gestures

Gesture refers to movements involving the upper body, especially the hands. Just as everyday gestures communicate thoughts like "Be quiet!" or "Come here," so gestures in Christian worship communicate. We could even say that gesture is formative. Jeremy Haselock argues that the common gestures in worship serve to affirm community and beliefs, help the assembly to focus on the words and actions of the service, and teach people to pray with their entire beings.[73] He categorizes gestures according to whether they (1) express the affections of worshippers, (2) express the relationship between assembly members and/or between the assembly and God, (3) symbolize, or (4) perform practical functions.[74] Described below are the most common gestures of liturgical leaders and assembly members.

Following the Jewish custom of standing with outstretched arms (Ps 141:2; 1 Tim 2:8), many worship leaders use the *orans* (Latin: "prayer") gesture, especially during important acts of prayer such as the collect (opening prayer) and the eucharistic prayer. Just as the hands are lifted upward, so the mind is directed "upward" to God in prayer. Orans was lost as a common gesture of the assembly, to be replaced in the Middle

73. Haselock, "Gestures," 228.
74. Haselock, "Gestures," 228.

Ages by the bowing of the head and folding of hands, which expresses reverence before a dignitary of feudal society.

The *laying on of hands*, mainly a clerical gesture, is associated with healing (Luke 4:40) and ordination (1 Tim 4:14). It symbolizes the conferral of power, authority, and spiritual gifts, and thus points to the transformative work of God in the church. Hand-laying continues to be used in rites of healing, ordination, and baptism. In baptismal rites, it is often administered with a prayer requesting the gifts of the Holy Spirit.[75]

Another gesture that requires the use of the minister's hand is the *imposition of ashes* on Ash Wednesday (the first day of the season of Lent). Typically, a mixture of palm ashes and oil are marked on a worshipper's head in the form of a cross. The action is accompanied by the words "Remember that you are dust, and to dust you shall return" (Gen 3:19). In the ancient world, the wearing of ashes symbolized mortality and repentance (Dan 9:3). Hence Christians impose ashes as a reminder of their need for redemption as they begin their spiritual journey toward Easter and the celebration of Jesus' redeeming passage from death to life.

Also customarily associated with clergy, the *blessing* gesture involves the raising of the hands to the level of the minister's head, with palms turned outward toward the liturgical assembly. Drawing on Jesus' action prior to the ascension (Luke 24:50), this gesture is typically used as the minister pronounces the "Aaronic blessing" (Num 6:24) or another blessing formula at the conclusion of a public worship service. In many liturgical traditions the minister makes the sign of the cross during the benediction to suggest that the blessings of the service—and indeed all blessings—come from Jesus Christ, the crucified one. The cross is traced in the air using the right hand, pointed upward with the palm facing to the left, moving from head to breast and from left shoulder to right shoulder.[76]

The *sign of the cross* is also used at other times by clergy and members of the worship assembly. Typically, at the mention of God's triune name, all worshippers trace the cross over themselves—forehead to breast, left shoulder to right shoulder—using the thumb and first two fingers of the right hand held together. Ministers may mark the sign of the cross on baptismal candidates to suggest ownership by Christ, or to anoint the

---

75. "Holy Baptism," *ELW*, 31.

76. In some Lutheran and Anglican churches, the presiding minister makes the sign of the cross over the communion elements during the eucharistic prayer, especially at the words "bless and sanctify." See Galley, *Ceremonies*, 114–16.

newly baptized with oil as an association with the Holy Spirit.[77] While not biblically mandated, the sign of the cross symbolizes the means of our redemption and reminds us of our baptism when we were joined with Christ in his death and resurrection.

Although the Bible associates the lifting of the hands with prayer, it is common today for many worshippers to lift (and wave) their hands during the worship (song) set of a contemporary worship service. The uplifting of the hands, in this instance, represents the praise of the worshippers going "up" to God as well as the "lifting up" or magnifying of God's name through the assembly's songs of praise. Many of the most beloved praise and worship songs include the words "lifting," "raising," and "high up," e.g., "Great is the Lord," and "Lord, I Lift Your Name on High."

Bowing is a sign of deep respect and humility (Ps 95:6), and today this gesture essentially serves as a replacement for prostration or genuflection (dropping down to one knee). Typically ministers and people bow when approaching the altar as an acknowledgment of the presence of Christ symbolized by the table. In some cases, ministers bow to each other as a means of greeting and mutual acknowledgement. In Asia, especially Japan, worshippers greet each other during the peace with a bow.

Processions

Movement of the entire body through space can be both informal as well as formal and stylized. The movement involved with leaving home to go to a service, although informal, is actually part of worship, because it represents the beginning of one's journey to encounter God. Upon arrival one makes one's way into the liturgical space, often to a favorite seat, which represents a coming into God's presence insofar as God is present in the space through words and actions that mediate that presence.

Processions are formal, organized movements of people to or within the place of worship. Liturgical processions to the Jerusalem temple that involved large numbers of people are mentioned in the psalms (42:4; 118:27). The ancient Roman church had processions of clergy and large throngs of Christians that traversed through the whole city, with stops for devotions at designated "stational" churches, before continuing to the church where the papal Eucharist was to take place. The most common type of procession in the church today is the entrance procession, which involves ministers

77. "Holy Baptism," *ELW*, 231.

moving through the midst of the assembly to take their appointed seats or places of leadership as the assembly sings the opening song. In the so-called liturgical churches (e.g., Anglican, Lutheran), there is a hierarchical arrangement whereby lay ministers precede ordained professional clergy, the chief of whom (the "presider") is last in the procession.[78] Ministers will leave the worship space in procession (a "recessional") in the same order both for the utilitarian purpose of departing from the worship space and to symbolize the whole assembly's movement from the worship service back into the world for everyone's ministry in daily life. The liturgical processions of the Sunday service, in a larger sense, symbolize the pilgrim journey of God's people making their way through this world to the final consummation of God's redemptive reign, much like the people of Israel journeyed through the wilderness to the promised land.

In some churches the ministers will process into the midst of the assembly for the reading of the gospel lesson, the culminating Scripture lesson appointed for a Sunday or feast day. This action heightens the importance of the gospel and symbolizes the church's movement into the world to proclaim the good news.

Occasional services also involve processions. In the marriage rite, the procession of the bride and groom to the area before the altar is common even in nonliturgical, less formalistic churches. Besides simply getting the participants to their proper places, the wedding procession recalls the ancient custom whereby the groom led a procession to the home of the bride for the purpose taking her to his own home for the marriage feast.[79] Funerals have long involved a procession to the place of burial accompanied by the singing of psalms. Although funeral processions in industrialized societies often involve driving by automobile to a cemetery located some distance from the church (or funeral home), the movement still symbolizes the journey that all Christians are making to the grave and ultimately to the resurrection from the dead.

78. This arrangement reflects Jesus' teaching on the servant nature of Christian leadership and his saying that "many who are first will be last, and the last first" (Mark 9:35; 10:31).

79. See chapter 4, "Life Cycle Rituals in the Old Testament, Marriage."

Space

All of the components of Christian ritual come together in particular places, whether they are called churches, temples, or meetings houses. Before we can talk about the setting of the church's ritual actions, we must distinguish between *sacred space* and *liturgical space*. The former is usually connected with a supernatural event, e.g., the appearance of God or a holy person. In other words, a sacred space is a place of *theophany* (the manifestation of God). In the Old Testament, for example, Bethel became a sacred location because of Jacob's wrestling match there with an angel, an event that he memorialized by constructing an altar and consecrating it with a libation (Gen 35:14–15). Places associated with the life and ministry of Jesus (e.g., the Lake of Gennesaret, the Mount of Olives in Jerusalem) are regarded as holy by Christians. Roman Catholics revere those places where the Virgin Mary appeared to one or more individuals (e.g., Fatima in Portugal, Lourdes in France, and Medjugorje in Bosnia and Herzegovina). These places have become popular pilgrimage destinations both for purposes of learning and physical healing.

In addition to the ritualistic act of making their way to such places, pilgrims will also engage in prayer, meditation, and participation in worship services at pilgrimage sites. For Protestants places such as the City Church (Stadt Kirche) in Wittenberg, Germany, where Martin Luther preached, or (John) Wesley's Chapel (City Road Chapel, London) are "sacred" because of their association with a revered preacher-Reformer. In some sense, these places have become pilgrimage sites with numerous visitors each year, although some Protestants reject the whole idea of pilgrimage, believing that it is bound up with false beliefs about saints and "superstitions." They would suggest that such places only hold historical interest and no more.

A *liturgical space* is one specifically designed and used for Christian public worship and its associated rituals. The precursors of Christian liturgical spaces are those worship structures used by the ancient Jews: the tabernacle, the Jerusalem temple, and the synagogue. The tabernacle used during the wilderness journey and the Jerusalem temple were places for encountering God through sacrificial acts. God promises to speak to Moses in the tabernacle, and this will effectively be *the* place where God meets the whole community of Israel (Exod 29:42–46). Additionally, God promises to be present in the tabernacle to receive the daily sacrificial offerings:

> Then the LORD said to Moses, "Command the Israelites and say
> to them: See that you present to Me at its appointed time the
> food for My offerings by fire, as a pleasing aroma to Me. And
> tell them that this is the offering made by fire you are to present
> to the LORD as a regular burnt offering each day: two unblem-
> ished year-old male lambs. Offer one lamb in the morning and
> the other at twilight, along with a tenth of an ephah of fine flour
> as a grain offering, mixed with a quarter hin of oil from pressed
> olives. (Num 28:1–5)

Later, God promises Solomon to always be present in the Jerusalem
temple:

> Now when Solomon had finished building the house of the LORD
> and the royal palace, and had achieved all that he had desired to
> do, the LORD appeared to him a second time, as He had appeared
> to him at Gibeon. And the LORD said to him:

> "I have heard your prayer and petition before Me. I have conse-
> crated this temple you have built by putting My Name there forev-
> er; My eyes and My heart will be there for all time." (1 Kgs 9:1–3)

While the temple was a unique edifice found only in Jerusalem and
was dedicated to sacrificial acts, the synagogue, a development of the
exilic era, served as a house of prayer and biblical instruction for Jewish communities wherever they were located. Jesus himself frequently
taught in the synagogues of Galilee (Matt 9:35), and Paul spoke in many
synagogues during his various missionary journeys (Acts 14:1). Both the
Lord and his apostle found the synagogue a genial place to carry out their
respective missions.

Like the tabernacle/temple, the Christian liturgical space is a place
of encounter with God. As the locus of Word and sacrament, it is where
Jesus himself speaks to the assembly through the proclaimed word (Luke
10:16; cf. Luke 24:27), and is made known in the breaking of the bread,
that is, the Lord's Supper (Luke 24:35). Early Christians believed that the
celebration of the Lord's Supper itself consecrated a space, that is, dedicated it as a ritual space. This suggests that, for Christians, the "holiness"
of a liturgical space derives from the actions performed there. Indeed,
we could say that, through our holy actions, a liturgical space becomes
a sacred space. We are challenged, therefore, to thoughtfully design our
liturgical spaces so that they not only facilitate the holy actions of the
sacraments but also witness to the sacredness of these actions through the

proper placement of the liturgical centers, and the inspiring use of color, light, ard architectural decoration.

In the manner of the Jewish synagogue, a Christian liturgical space is for the prayer and instruction (Act 2:42) of a gathered assembly of worshippers. As such, it is a place for people, rather than a shrine for the deity (as in the ancient, pre-Christians religions). Accordingly, Christian liturgical spaces are designed with adequate lighting, acoustics, movement space, and unobstructed sight lines to the central liturgical structures (e.g., the communion table, pulpit, and baptismal font).[80]

It has to be admitted, however, that the New Testament has little to say about the spaces used for early Christian worship. Many acts of worship take place in the outdoors, such as Jesus' preaching and his feeding a crowd of five thousand people. Jesus himself was baptized in the Jordan River, and the first baptisms were presumably administered outdoors (Acts 2:41), as was certainly the case with the Ethiopian eunuch (Acts 8:26–40). Likewise, much of the preaching in the New Testament occurred in the outdoors (Matt 5:1; Acts 2:14). Interestingly, when Jesus celebrates a Passover meal with his disciples using an indoor space, only a few physical details are shared (Mark 14:15).

The lack of prescription concerning sacred and liturgical spaces in the New Testament may reflect the church's understanding that Jesus himself is a new temple, that is to say, the means of encountering God (John 2:19, 21). At the same time, the Christian community is viewed as a new temple where God "dwells" (1 Cor 3:16–17; 1 Pet 2:4–5). Since Jesus and his people constitute a new temple, it is not surprising that the New Testament has little to say about sacred/liturgical spaces. In any event, since early Christians believed in the imminent return of Jesus to establish the new Jerusalem, any discussion about physical space was moot. At most, we can only say that the New Testament affirms a need for Christians to gather for worship in designated spaces.

But we can find a theological rationale for liturgical space in the doctrine of the incarnation (John 1:14; Phil 2:7). God's act of encountering us through a flesh-and-blood person, Jesus, affirms not only the goodness of the human body but also the worthiness of meeting the needs of the body, particularly the need to have organized spaces where it can engage in rituals. We need not apologize for constructing spaces that are suitable for human interactions involving sights, sounds, and the physical movement

---

80. See White and White, *Church Architecture*, 21–35, and Truscott, *Worship*, 96–97.

of people. The gospel, after all, is shared in a human world and through human means, and God is not ashamed to meet us in this earthly, fleshly world, with all its limitations and possibilities.

In saying that the design of a Christian liturgical space, as a reflection of the incarnation, should take human needs and limitations into consideration, I do not mean to suggest that Christian liturgical architecture is averse to aesthetic considerations. Our study of brain neurobiology has suggested that color, decoration, and images all impact the brain and effect the emotions, creating an ambience of mystery and awe that enable worshippers to enter into the liturgy in a spirit of reverence. Accordingly, Christians strive to achieve a balance between functionality and aesthetics, so that a space facilitates the necessary liturgical actions while fostering devotion.

Sacred Art

Christians design and build places for worship and then adorn them with works of art.

But before we can discuss art in liturgical spaces, we must distinguish between two terms. *Sacred art* is a broad category that refers to works with religious subjects. This could include anything from the paintings on the ceiling of the Sistine Chapel in Rome, to depictions of Jesus and his disciples in Sunday school books for children. A jewel-encrusted cross of gold on a cathedral altar or a simple cross worn around a person's neck could also be considered sacred art. In contrast to sacred art is *liturgical* or *ritual art*—objects that are created for use in the spaces where public worship services are held.[81] If it is true that the prehistoric depictions of animals on the caves of Chauvet, France—representations of shamanistic visions— summoned "spirits" to aid Paleolithic humans in various life endeavors,[82] then the Christian use of art for religious/devotional purposes is something that we share in common with the rest of humanity.

Within the history of Israel, there seems to have been an evolution of thought on the legitimacy of images and other forms of representational art in liturgical spaces and elsewhere. On the one hand, the ark of the covenant was decorated with two cherubim (Exod 25:22), and a bronze serpent was put on top of a pole in order that snake bite victims might gaze

81. White, *Introduction*, 103–4.

82. Hammer, "Finally, the Beauty of France's Chauvet Cave," para. 14.

upon it and be healed (Num 21:9). But, on the other hand, the so-called "deuteronomistic reformation" of the seventh century BCE brought with it an absolute prohibition against sacred images (Exod 20:4–5). The latter development probably represents a reaction against the religion of neighboring nations with their long history of producing images and statues of their various deities. Since the worship and devotion of these ancient religions were orientated toward artistic images, outlawing images effectively outlawed the religion.

Early Christian sensibilities about art and images reflect the Old Testament struggle. Statues were avoided because of the Old Testament prohibition against "graven images," i.e., three-dimensional representations in stone or wood (Exod 20:4; Deut 7:5). Moreover, statues would have been confusing to converts who had left behind pagan religions with their various statues and idols of the gods. Painting was deemed more suitable for Christians because it avoided the connotations of the pagan cult and because vibrant colors painted on surfaces made buildings come alive, while the images that depicted biblical stories and core doctrines reinforced verbal instruction. Theological opinion in the early church, however, was actually divided between those authors who encouraged artistic depictions (Gregory the Great) and those who discouraged them for various reasons (Tertullian, Jerome).[83]

Given the tensions over sacred art in the early church, the iconoclastic controversies of the eighth and ninth centuries in the Christian East were perhaps inevitable. Although the use of icons (images of Christ and the saints) was well established in both private and public worship by this time, iconoclasts condemned religious images and advocated a ban on their use in home and church. They argued that images violated Old Testament prohibitions and, since images were one with the "prototype" or thing depicted, they were fake gods, and thus idols to be eschewed. It is notable that the controversy began in the eastern Mediterranean and that it occurred *after* the rise of Islam, with its strict opposition to images.

The "orthodox" defenders of images were led by John of Damascus (676–749), who argued that since God became visible in the person of Jesus, God's likeness (as Jesus the Son of God) could be depicted in art.[84] Furthermore, John distinguished between the honoring of images—similar to the honoring of persons of high social status—and the adoration

---

83. Dawtry, "Art and Worship," 28.

84. John of Damascus, *First Apology* (early eighth century), para. 8.

that is given to God alone.[85] Contrary to the claim of iconoclasts, John noted that there is a distinction between a thing and a depiction of that thing; he points out, for example, how the drawing of a man does not possess the mental powers of a man.[86] Because iconoclasts refused to venerate images, John accuses them of Manichaeism, a dualistic religion that tended to equate matter and material things with evil. Eventually, the iconophiles (those favoring icons) triumphed and were able to promote the veneration of icons, albeit with a kind of "relative worship" whereby the reverence offered to the icon "passed through" and was received by the prototype (the holy person depicted in the icon).

The Middle Ages saw a flowering of art, especially in the great cathedrals of Northern Europe. The wealth generated by the rise of international commerce made it possible for rulers and merchants to fund large, architecturally intricate churches and to adorn these with tapestries, statues, paintings, and stained glass windows. Paintings and statues of saints gave worshippers a profound and realistic sense of being surrounded by a cloud of witnesses (Heb 12:1). The growing affluence of the age as well as its sacramental piety was evident in eucharistic vessels, especially patens and chalices, which were forged from silver and gold and inlaid with rubies, emeralds, and other gemstones. Satin and silk with interwoven threads of gold were fashioned into eucharistic vestments worn by the ministers for the daily masses, especially masses for the dead. The ruling elite of a community were entombed in or near elaborate chantry chapels, where masses beseeching God for their eternal rest were celebrated.

The Protestant Reformation, however, witnessed a resurgence of iconoclasm, especially in Switzerland, Germany, and England. Protestant iconoclasts viewed artistic depictions as diverting attention away from the Word of God. Iconography of saints was especially proscribed because the invocation of saints lacked a biblical basis and tended to deny Christ's unique role in humanity's salvation (1 Tim 2:5; Heb 9:15). Unfortunately, Protestant iconoclasm in the sixteenth century was often violent and even led to the destruction of pipe organs. Although he argued that images ultimately did not serve God and could be a matter of abuse, Martin Luther nevertheless opposed their forceful destruction. He believed that images should be retained because they potentially aided the faith of some people.[87] During Luther's

---

85. John of Damascus, *First Apology*, para. 8.

86. John of Damascus, *Third Apology*, para. 17.

87. Luther, *Eight Sermons at Wittenberg* (1522), *LW* 51:84–85.

lifetime, the painter Lucas Cranach the Elder (ca. 1472–1553) provided altar pieces for a number of Lutheran churches, including the city church in Wittenberg where Luther himself preached frequently. Cranach also contributed illustrations for Luther's translation of the Bible.

While churches of the past were awash with art, and were even major patrons of the arts, this is hardly the case today. Doubtless influenced by iconoclastic voices of the past and utilitarian attitudes of the present, contemporary churches rarely commission works of art for their liturgical spaces. Frugality and a desire to avoid any sense of elitism may also play a role in the near banishment of art from the modern church building. Many of the so-called "liturgical" churches, however, do have furnishings with artistic symbols, e.g., altars with images of eucharistic cups or stalks of wheat, or baptismal fonts with images of crosses or doves (to represent the Holy Spirit). Such churches also use banners, paraments (cloth hangings for altars and pulpits), and eucharistic vessels with symbolic images crafted by professional artists. Perhaps because of its long history, beauty, and inspirational value, stained glass has retained a place in many churches today.

What, then, is the purpose of art in the Christian liturgy and life? Traditionally, stained glass and other art forms were thought to have a pedagogical function, namely, to teach Bible stories to uneducated laypeople. Arguably, however, Christian ritual art has to do with more than cognitive "knowledge." By depicting Jesus and various biblical persons, art enables the biblical world to become part of this world. Art, in other words, incarnates the heavenly realm, the kingdom of God, such that we identify with the persons and situations depicted and thus perceive that the gospel message in the artwork is relevant to our own world. For example: people of the Middle Ages, whose lives were under constant stress due to hunger, disease, and warfare, would have found comfort and reassurance in depictions of Jesus' crucifixion and resurrection because these suggest the possibility of deliverance from suffering.

In terms of brain neurology, the colors of stained glass attract the eye and stimulate the parts of the brain that deal with emotions,[88] thus drawing the viewer into the depiction in a very personal way. The content of stained-glass windows depicting Jesus' passage from death to life offered medieval Christians a "solution" to their earthly troubles and thereby activated the quiescent system, giving a sense of assurance and enabling them to carry on with everyday activities. Perhaps art has lost its significance

88 Bailey, "How Colors Affect Human Behavior," para. 6–9.

for modern humans because medicine, psychology, and technology have all become ways of solving life's problems. But none of these "solutions," unlike art, can stimulate our imaginations so that we are drawn into the spiritual realm where we can ponder life's quandaries from a more transcendent perspective. We might therefore hope that art will always have a place in Christian worship—even if a diminished one.

Conclusion

In concluding this chapter, I must stress that all of the components of ritual described above do not exist in isolation, whether in the Christian church or in any other faith tradition. Rather, they together constitute a ritual system. But why a ritual system? Would not just sacred story, for example, be enough to form people into a faith community?

By way of response, it must be pointed out that the church is a culture, a unique society with its own ways and values. As we know, any culture has a multiplicity of components that together form people according to its ways and values. No one component of culture can bear the entire formational task due to the complexity of the human person and the uniqueness of individuals. So it is with the church, whose complex ritual system forms us into the people of Jesus Christ. The authors and compilers of the various biblical books, and the faith communities for whom they labored, were well aware of the role that ritual systems played in faith formation. Accordingly, our next chapter will provide an overview of ritual in the Bible, so that we might better appreciate how Christian spiritual formation through ritual has its roots in the Bible and the earliest Christian communities.

Chapter 4

Ritual in the Bible

Introduction

IN PREVIOUS CHAPTERS WE discussed the purposes of ritual: (1) to induce heightened awareness or "unitary states" whereby a person experiences awe and the presence of transcendent powers (brain chemistry); (2) to enable beliefs to be experienced by the body; (3) to enact sacred stories so that worshippers can find resolution to life's questions, problems, and ambiguities; (4) to ease a person through life transitions that can otherwise cause anxiety (cultural anthropology); and (5) to "know" by means of the body (performance theory). These are all at work in the rituals described in the Bible. In some cases, ceremonial details may be lacking in the biblical literature, but it is clear that ritual activity was part of the life of both Judaic and Christian communities. This chapter will offer a survey of ritual in the Bible and reflect on how rituals shaped the religious awareness of the people who experienced them. It is not meant as an exhaustive study of ritual in the Bible. Such would be impossible since biblical authors wrote to address specific issues involving rituals, rather than to provide complete catalogues of the rituals in their communities. But it is my belief that the Bible demonstrates how ritual is inherent to the existence of faith communities.

Ritual in the Old Testament

Sacrifice and Sacrificial Offerings in the Old Testament

Sacrifice is one of the most basic acts of worship in the Old Testament. Ancient Israel had collective memories of sacrifices that occurred even before the official sacrifices of the tabernacle or temple.[1] Thus offering something of one's own is a ritual act that predates "cultic" or "liturgical" worship with its appointed ministers or priests, vestments, days, times, seasons, and collections of sacred songs (hymns). It is fitting, then, to begin the discussion of ritual in the Bible with what may be one of humanity's first ritual responses to the encounter with God.

Israel's literature depicts sacrifice taking place even before Moses. Cain and Abel both presented offerings to the Lord (Gen 4:3–5). Abel's offering ("fat portions from some of the first born of his flock") was more acceptable to the Lord because the selectiveness suggested sincerity, gratitude, and a deeper appreciation for human dependence on God.[2] Noah sacrificed to God "from every kind of clean animal and clean bird" (Gen 8:20), apparently as an act of thanksgiving for the cessation of the flood. The result was that the Lord promised to never again curse the ground or to destroy living creatures (Gen 8:21), as if Noah's sacrifice atoned for human wickedness and propitiated God's wrath.

The patriarchs built sacrificial altars, beginning with those constructed by Abram at Shechem and Bethel (Gen 12:7, 8). The story of Abraham's aborted sacrifice of his son Isaac—intriguing if somewhat disturbing—draws attention to the relationship between sacrifice and the inner disposition of the offerer: God spares Abraham the task of killing his only son because Abraham's willingness to do so revealed his faith (Gen 22:12; Jas 2:21–23). According to the Letter to the Hebrews, it was this faith that made him right in God's eyes (11:17). Like Abram, Jacob also built an altar (Gen 35:7), and later sacrificed (Gen 46:1) on the eve of his sojourn into Egypt, cementing his relationship with God at a pivotal moment in his life.

The regulations concerning sacrificial offerings in the Pentateuch (the Five Books of Moses) are quite precise in their requirements. The animal offered had to belong to the person making the offering, i.e., be domesticated rather than wild. In addition, it was to be "clean." In almost all cases, the animal had to be perfect, without any blemish or defect (Lev 22:17–25), and be at least eight days old. If there was a sacrificial meal, the fat and blood of the animal could not be consumed, but had to be burned on the altar. The most commonly used animals were lambs, cattle,

1. Genesis 4 mentions the offerings of Cain and Abel, the former of which was rejected by God. Later in Genesis 22, Abraham sacrifices a ram provided by God in lieu of his son Isaac.

2. Hebrews 11:4 suggests that Abel's offering was acceptable to God because it was done in faith and thus bespoke his righteousness.

rams, and goats, although sheep and oxen were also used. The principal sacrifices were as follows:

The *burnt offering* involved the complete incineration of the sacrificed animal (Lev 1). To symbolize the animal's role as his representative, the offerer laid his hands on it after presenting it to the priest. The victim's blood was thrown against the altar to symbolize God's participation in the event. Then followed the burning of the entire animal on the altar by the priest. The actions created an aroma that was pleasing to God, thus placating God and atoning for the sin.

The *cereal offering* (Lev 2:6, 14–18) had two parts. First was the portion that was burned on the altar in order to represent the offerer and his intentions to God. The remaining part was consumed by the priests and was considered the most holy part. Salt was added, perhaps as a symbol of purity. Cereal offerings were made in conjunction with animal offerings, especially the burnt offering. Usually, the offering took the form of flour that had oil poured on it and incense placed on top of it.

The *peace* or *fellowship offering* (Lev 3; 7:11–36) was a burnt offering that gave a pleasing aroma to God. Unlike the burnt offering, some parts of the animal were reserved for consumption by the priests and the offerer(s) in a common meal. The three subcategories of peace offerings were: (1) the thank offering, consisting of both cereal and animal offerings given as an expression of thanks for a blessing from God, followed by the consumption of the animal on the same day; (2) the votive offering, which signified gratitude for either a divine blessing or deliverance from trouble following a vow made by the offerer; and (3) the freewill offering, which served as an expression of thanks without the offerer having received a blessing or deliverance. Because minor flaws were allowed in the animal presented for a freewill offering (Lev 22:23), God's acceptance of the offering was based on the sincerity of the offerer rather than the quality of the offering.

The *sin offering* (Lev 4:1–5:13), made in order to atone for unintentional sins, appears similar to the guilt offering, except that specific offerings were assigned according to who committed the sin, whether a priest the entire congregation, the king, or one of the common people. For example, while the priest had to offer a young bull, the commoner was required to offer a female goat. Allowance was made for sacrificial offerings by those unable to afford a lamb or goat. Some of the blood was to be sprinkled before the sanctuary curtain, another portion applied to the horns of the altar of incense, and the rest was poured out at the base of the altar of offering. Fat was cut away from the liver and kidneys and burned on the altar, while the rest of the animal was burned in a ceremonially clean area outside the camp. The priest who offered the animal could eat its flesh in a holy place (Lev 6:26).

The *guilt offering* (Lev 5:14–6:7), although similar to the sin offering in some ways, was different in that it required restitution for any loss to the holy things of the Lord or any loss to the priests. When damage was done against another person, there was to be restitution in full to the owner plus one-fifth of the value. The offering served to atone for the sin and brought forgiveness to the offerer.

Besides those sacrifices that atoned for sin or gave thanks, there were also regular sacrifices. These took place daily, in the morning and evening (Exod 29:38–42), and on most of the major yearly festivals: Unleavened Bread (Num 28:16–25), Weeks/Pentecost (Num 28:26–31), First Fruits (Lev 23:9–14), the New Year/Trumpets (Num 29:1–6), the Day of Atonement (Num 29:7–11), and the Feast of Booths (Num 28:12–38), whose volume of offerings exceeded that of any other holy assembly. Sacrifices were also made on an "as-needed" basis for the purification of women (Lev 12:1–8), the cleansing of lepers (Lev 14:1–32), and the consecration of priests.

Sacrifice, as a form of ritual, might be interpreted in light of our previous discussion of brain neurobiology and its relationship to the experience of God. Needless to say, sacrifice was a spectacle for the senses. The sight of blood being poured on the altar and the odors of burning animal flesh and incense undoubtedly evoked fear and awe. Coupled with the teaching that God dwelled in the midst of Israel (as symbolized by the ark of the covenant in the tabernacle/temple), and further heightened by music and bodily movements, sacrifice may well have brought about a unitary state, i.e., a mystical/transcendent experience. If nothing else, sacrifice enabled the concepts of "atonement," "thanksgiving," and "fellowship with God" to be experienced in concrete, bodily ways—one "ate" thanksgiving and fellowship.

Sacrifice as a religious act undoubtedly strikes the modern person as strange, antiquated, and irrational, especially when it comes to atoning sacrifices. But it might help to think of sacrifice as a means for negotiating the divine-human relationship, much like human relationships involve the giving and receiving of goods and money in order to establish and maintain relationships. In the Old Testament, the divine-human relationship was established by a covenant, and it required faithfulness and obedience on the part of Israel. Atoning sacrifices were meant to restore the relationship between the community of Israel and God, or between an individual and God, when sin destroyed the relationship by evoking God's wrath. These, however, were not to be offered in a perfunctory manner, but with sincerity and purity of heart. In other words, the offerer had to recognize that he had offended God and needed to make amends by surrendering something of himself to God. By laying hands on the sacrificial victim, the offerer personally identifies with it, making it *his* offering and dedicating it to a holy purpose. Atonement occurs because the blood cleanses away the offerer's sin (Heb 9:22)[3] and the burning of the animal signifies the offerer's giving his whole self to God in rededication. But since the Old Testament regards all things as properly "belonging" to God (1 Chron 29:14), sacrificing means surrendering control of something back to God—an act of confessing God's sovereignty over the offerer and his possessions.

Besides repentance, self-surrender, and rededication to God, sacrifice also expressed an offerer's thanks to God. For the ancient Israelites (not unlike many modern people) gratitude was something to be embodied—indeed, we might say that for them gratitude was not gratitude unless it was embodied. Performance theory helps us to understand that Israel's sacrificial offerings (the action and thing offered) are not only the visible manifestation of thanks, but *are* the thanks. Just as many people today cannot conceive of their gratitude as taking any other form than a card with a handwritten note, so the ancient Israelites gave something of themselves to God when an expression of thanks seemed appropriate.

Sacred Spaces in the Old Testament

While the Jerusalem temple was the premier sacred space of the Old Testament, it was not Israel's first space designated for ritual. Even during the wilderness journey following the exodus, Israel had sacred spaces. At first, there was a provisional tent of meeting, placed outside the camp. Moses would enter the tent to speak with God, whose presence appeared as a pillar of cloud at the tent's entrance. The sight evoked awe and worship from

---

3. In the Old Testament, there is the understanding that blood is needed to atone for sin because "whoever sheds human blood, by humans shall their blood be shed" (Gen 9:6). This essentially means that death (the shedding of blood) is the penalty for sin. Under the law of Moses, animal blood was used vicariously in sin offerings to remit sin. Hence it is said that blood "cleanses" from sin. Gehman, "Blood," 121.

the Israelites (Exod 33:7–11). The tabernacle, by contrast, was a portable sanctuary placed inside the camp, and the divine cloud rested not outside of it but inside it (Exod 40:34–35). Once Israel came to inhabit Canaan, the tabernacle (tent of meeting) was brought successively to Shiloh (Josh 18:1), Nob (1 Sam 21), Gibeon (1 Chr 16:39), and finally to the temple in Jerusalem (1 Kings 8:4).

The tabernacle served as a depository for the tablets of the law and as a meeting place between God and the people of Israel. The interior contained two compartments, one referred to as "the holy place" and the other as the "holy of holies." In the latter was placed the ark of the covenant (Exod 25:10–22), which was topped by a slab of gold with a cherub resting at each end. It was here that the blood of sacrificed animals was sprinkled to effect propitiation for sins. In the holy place was an altar for the burning of incense. Off to one side stood the table for the Bread of the Presence (aka "showbread"), twelve loaves of bread that were replenished every Sabbath after the old ones were eaten by the priests. The twelve loaves thus arranged in the holy place (i.e., in the presence of God) served to remind Israel that it lived always in the presence of God who was its constant provider of food and other necessities.[4] On the opposite side stood a lampstand made of pure gold (Exod 25:31–40) with six branches, all of which were at the same height as the central shaft. Olive oil burned in the lamps throughout the night into the morning, symbolizing the continuous worship of God and the unending "light" to be given off by the people of Israel.[5]

Surrounding the tabernacle was a courtyard that was bounded with linen screens, as if to demarcate the holy space. On the entrance side of the tabernacle was a copper-covered altar used for burnt sacrifices (Exod 27:1–8). Between the altar and entrance was a "laver"—essentially a water-filled copper basin used by the priests for washing sacrificial vessels.

From a theological standpoint, the tabernacle is essentially a dwelling place for God on earth. Its construction according to God's own specifications meant that it conveyed the spiritual realities of the time to the Israelites.[6] Because the ark of the covenant was the place where God manifested himself (Exod 25:22), the implication was that the law itself was a revelation of God. The veil and the antechamber symbolized the utter holiness of God, since Aaron was not to move beyond these into the

4. Freeman, "Showbread," 1098.

5. Gehman, "Candlestick," 142.

6. Gooding, "Tabernacle," 1145–47.

holy of holies at will (Lev 16:2). The incense altar represented the prayers of the people going up to God (Ps 141:2). The laver, used for ceremonial handwashing, suggested the need for purity on the part of God's ministers (Exod 30:20), while the copper altar and the place of burnt offerings symbolized reconciliation between God and humans and served as the place for those actions that effected this reconciliation.

After Israel's entrance into the land of Canaan, a number of sacred places were utilized. In the days of the Judges, there was a shrine in the hill country of Ephraim, but its sacred objects and priests were taken to Laish-Dan by the Danites in order to establish a rival sanctuary (Judg 17, 18). Prior to the time of Samuel, there was a sanctuary at Shiloh where sacrifices were made (1 Samuel 1:3, 7), and in David's time Ahimelek served as a priest at a sanctuary where the "bread of the presence" was kept (1 Sam 21:1–8). Solomon sacrificed at a shrine at Gibeon, where God had appeared to him in a dream (1 Kgs 3:4–5). Still later, Jeroboam I established shrines at Dan and Bethel in the Northern Kingdom of Israel to serve as rivals to the temple in Jerusalem (1 Kgs 12:28–33)—even setting up golden calves in these sanctuaries.

The first of Jerusalem's three temples was constructed under King Solomon (1 Kgs 6 and 7), although it was King David who gathered the necessary materials, e.g., gold, silver, stone, and wood (1 Chron 29). The entire interior was overlaid with gold and was decorated with carved cherubim and depictions of vegetation, which suggested paradise. At the east end was the holy of holies, which contained the ark of the covenant, placed under the wings of two massive cherubim of carved wood. A wooden partition, covered with gold, separated the holy of holies and the holy place. There were golden chains drawn across the front of the holy of holies, but no curtain, as mentioned in 2 Chronicles 3:14. The holy place contained a wooden altar for the daily offering of incense. There was also a multibranched lampstand and ten tables for the showbread. The temple proper was surrounded by a three-story building used for storage and chambers for the various temple officials. There was a portico and vestibule with two bronze pillars that were ornamented. Immediately outside the temple was the court of the priests (2 Chron 4:9) where stood the sacrificial altar (1 Kgs 8:64). Nearby were ten bronze lavers and the "molten sea," a large water receptacle also made of bronze mounted on twelve bronze oxen. While the former was used to wash the various offerings, the latter was used for the priests to wash themselves.[7]

7. https://www.biblegateway.com/resources/encyclopedia-of-the-bible/Molten-Sea.

Outside the entrance leading to the altar was the court of Israel (i.e., the "court of men") and beyond that, at a lower level, was the court of the women. The temple was destroyed when the city was captured and burned by the Babylonians in 586 BCE.[8]

The second, or Zerubbabel's, temple was begun in the second year after the return from Babylonian captivity and completed in the sixth year of Darius, king of Babylon, ca. 515 BCE (Ezra 3:8; 6:15). This temple was planned on a much smaller scale but also utilized wood and precious metals in the construction. The building was paid for by the freewill offerings of the people. Many of the vessels of the former temple were restored (Ezra 1:7–11), but the ark of the covenant disappeared after the destruction of the first temple. The sanctuary was furnished with an incense altar, a lampstand, and a table for the showbread. Outside stood a "sea of bronze" (a water receptacle) and the altar of sacrifice, which was constructed of stone (Sir 50:3). The whole temple and its precincts were enclosed by doors and gates.[9]

Twice as large as its immediate predecessor, the third temple ("Herod's Temple") was started in 20–19 BCE and completed in 62–64 CE. Many of the buildings were much higher than those of Solomon's Temple. The holy of holies and the sanctuary were laid out in the customary fashion, except that the former was separated from the latter by a veil. As usual, the holy place contained a golden altar for incense, tables for the showbread, and a lampstand. Surrounded by three-story buildings on the sides and the rear, the temple was entered through a large doorway with golden doors. The sacrificial altar outside the temple was constructed of uncut stones and was reached by an inclined plane. There was also a laver for the various washings that took place in connection with the sacrifices. All three of the courts (priest's, men's, women's) were enclosed and non-Israelites ("Gentiles") were only permitted into the outermost court ("court of the Gentiles"). This court was itself surrounded by walls with their various gates.[10]

Essentially, the temple served as a place for the people of Israel to meet God, for God "dwelled" in the temple by means of his mysterious divine presence that appeared in the holy of holies. It is important to note that while the people were on the move, God was on the move with

8. Gehman, "Temple," 930–31; Millard, "Temple," 1156–57; Westerholm, "Temple," 760–65.

9. Gehman, "Temple," 931–32; Millard, "Temple," 1158; Westerholm, "Temple," 768–70.

10. Gehman, "Temple," 932–34; Millard, "Temple," 1158; Westerholm, "Temple," 770–76.

them, and when Israel established itself as a nation, God established his presence in Zion—although God stipulated that only a holy people dare come to encounter him at that place. It would be here at the temple—and nowhere else—that God would receive the sacrifices that mediated and maintained Israel's relationship with God. Besides serving as a symbol of national unity and a place for sacrifice, the temple was also a liturgical space; various psalms describe acts of worship such as singing and praying taking place within the environs of the temple:

> Make a joyful noise to the LORD,
>> all the earth.
> Serve the LORD with gladness;
>> come into His presence with joyful songs.
> Know that the LORD is God.
>> It is He who made us, and we are His;
>> we are His people, and the sheep of His pasture.
> Enter His gates with thanksgiving
>> and His courts with praise;
>> give thanks to Him and bless His name.
> For the LORD is good,
>> and His loving devotion endures forever;
>> His faithfulness continues to all generations. (Ps 100)

We should note, finally, that the architecture of the temple served to heighten its sacredness. Starting from the east entrance, the areas (courts) became progressively higher, with the holy of holies being located at the highest part of the complex. The walls with their various doors and gates not only served to demarcate the holy versus the unholy, and the holy versus the holier, but also gave an aura of concealment that heightened the sense of mystery and "set-apartness." The massive size of doors and pillars, the carvings and generous use of gold and other precious metals, likewise suggested something set apart from everyday life. The various enclosures and stairways leading to ever holier areas would have evoked a sense of awe from the common worshipper, whereas for the priestly actors, the journey through the richly decorated holy place amid clouds of incense wafting through shafts of light may well have produced altered states of consciousness. While many Christian worship spaces today seem sparse and lacking in symbols, the mystery and sacrality of the Jerusalem temple invite us to ponder how our liturgical spaces can draw people beyond the everyday in order to experience the wonder and mystery of God.

The synagogue (Gk., "place of meeting") seems to have arisen in Babylon during the period of the exile.[11] Essentially, the synagogue was a place for studying the Scriptures and praying. In the time of Jesus, synagogues were found throughout the ancient world in just about every city that had a Jewish community, e.g., Antioch (Acts 13:14), Beroea (Acts 17:10), Damascus (Acts 9:2, 20), Thessalonika (Acts 17:1), Athens (Acts 17:17), Corinth (Acts 18:4), and Ephesus (Acts 18:19). Large cities such as Jerusalem and Alexandria had several synagogues (Acts 6:9).

The services were conducted by competent lay members of the community, although recognized teachers were permitted to offer instruction as well (Luke 4). The New Testament indicates that Jesus himself regularly taught in synagogues (Matt 4:23; 9:35; John 18:20), as did Paul (Acts 9:20; 13:15; 14:1; 19:8). Worship was held every Sabbath and on the second and fifth days of the week when a portion of the law (Torah) was read. During the Sabbath service the lay leader prayed using the Shema (Deut 6:4–9), and some or all of the Eighteen Benedictions (prayers of intercession for various concerns). Several persons read the lesson from the law. At some services a prophetic lesson was read, and this was followed by a sermon that explained the reading and exhorted the hearers to faithful living.

Generally, synagogues were rectangular buildings that were oriented toward Jerusalem. The congregation assembled in the large open area in the middle of the building, while some seating in the form of low ledges along the inside perimeter of the wall was provided. Many synagogues were decorated with depictions of vegetation, humans, and animals. Some even had mosaics on the floors. The lessons were read from the bema or raised platform, on which there may have been a stone leader's chair. The assembly area had a reading desk, chairs for elders and wealthy members, and a closet for the scrolls containing the Scriptures.[12]

The synagogue represents a significant development in the ritual life of Judaism. While even during the temple's existence Scripture reading and instruction could take place outside of Jerusalem, the gathering of Jews in synagogues meant that public worship was no longer tied to this city only. Since prayers could be offered wherever God's people lived and gathered

---

11. It is debatable, however, whether there is even mention of a synagogue anywhere in the Old Testament.

12. Feinberg, "Synagogue," 1142–43; Gehman, "Synagogue," 915–17.

for worship, the theological implication is that God is present to hear those prayers. The synagogue thus represents a recovery of the theological understanding behind the tent of meeting/tabernacle, namely, that God is with the people of Israel wherever they might roam, as opposed to being bound to one locale. Furthermore, the existence of the synagogue suggests the understanding that public ritual is not legitimated by its location, but by the presence of a community that gathers to "call on the name of the Lord."

The Liturgical Calendar of the Old Testament

In a previous chapter we discussed how sacred time serves to recapitulate the sacred stories that shape a community's identity. The observance of sacred time was a way for Israel to confess what it believed about God's actions in history for both its benefit and for the whole world. The discussion below will begin with the most important aspects of Israel's time observance, namely, the yearly festivals, the sabbath, and daily prayer times, before considering the less frequently observed Sabbatical and Jubilee Years.

The Passover (Exod 12), celebrated on the fifteenth day of the month of Nisan, was essentially a remembrance of Israel's deliverance from slavery in Egypt. The observance began with the selection of a lamb several days prior, which was to be sufficient for one household, although neighbors could join a household that was too small for one lamb. On the fourteenth/fifteenth day of the same month, the lamb was to be slaughtered at twilight, roasted whole with bitter herbs, and eaten with unleavened bread. Any meat that was left over until the next morning was to be burned. The lamb was eaten with unleavened bread, which symbolizes purity and the haste with which the Israelites were to leave Egypt. Blood from the lamb was to be smeared on the door posts, originally as a way of averting God from the Israelite households when he came to kill the firstborn, this "passing over" being the origin of the feast's name. The blood ritual was carried out with a branch of hyssop, which symbolized purity, while the blood itself denotes expiation or the appeasement of God.[13] Prior to the destruction of the temple (70 CE), the Passover could only be celebrated in Jerusalem, since the lamb had to be slaughtered

---

13. It is thought that the duplicate Passover instructions in Deuteronomy 16 represent a later ritual practice. The lack of reference here to the blood ritual might suggest the suppression of this domestic action in order to focus on the slaughtering of the victim at the Jerusalem temple, i.e., the central sanctuary.

within the temple compound, and all Israelite males were required to be in Jerusalem for the festival. After the destruction of the temple in 70 CE, the Passover became an entirely domestic celebration.

Celebrated in conjunction with the consumption of a lamb was the Feast of Unleavened Bread (Exod 12:17–20), which lasted for seven days (14 to 21 Nisan). On the first day (the first full day after the lamb repast), all yeast was to be removed from homes, and the people were to assemble again on the seventh day. During the seven days, only unleavened bread was to be consumed. This feast likewise serves as a remembrance of the exodus because "it was on this day that [God] brought your divisions out of Egypt" (Exod 12:17).

It is very likely that the feasts of Passover and Unleavened Bread both predate Israel. The lamb rite probably belonged originally to nomadic herdsmen, who sacrificed a lamb to appease their god and to offer thanks for the new births that replenished the herd in the springtime. The days of unleavened bread were originally observed as a Canaanite agricultural festival to give thanks for the spring grain harvest. In both cases, older observances were coopted into the religious cult of Israel in order to share the primal sacred story. They were likely combined in Israelite practice because of their temporal proximity to each other.

The Feast of Weeks, or Pentecost (Lev 23:15–21), was the second of the three major pilgrimage festivals that obliged all Israelite males to appear before the Lord in Jerusalem (Deut 16:9–12). Occurring fifty full days after the Passover, it required the cessation of work and a grain offering of two leavened loaves of salted bread (Lev 23:17), which were presented along with freewill offerings. Essentially the Feast of Weeks was an occasion for offering thanks to God for the grain that would sustain the community for another year. Eventually it came to be understood as a time for renewing the covenant with God. Following the destruction of the temple, the focus shifted to expressing gratitude for the giving of the law to Moses on Mount Sinai, an event traditionally thought to have occurred fifty days after the Passover and exodus from Egypt.[14]

The Feast of Booths (Deut 16:13–15) was the last of the three pilgrimage festivals and also served as the second harvest festival. The name refers to the practice of people living in makeshift booths ("tabernacles") out in the open or on rooftops during the seven-day-long celebration (Lev 23:40-42), which began on the seventh day of the seventh month of Tishri and coincided with

14. Gehman, "Weeks, Feast of," 989–90.

the harvesting of grain, grapes, and olives. Although this culminating festival was agricultural in nature, it became a way of remembering the wilderness trek with its temporary dwelling places.

Every seventh or Jubilee year, when there was supposed to be no harvesting, the law of Moses was read. Eventually, an eighth day was added that involved a solemn assembly, the purpose being to close off the annual round of festivals rather than to evoke the tabernacle experience in the wilderness. Over time, additional ceremonies were included, such as a procession around the altar with people carrying branches and fruit to the accompaniment of psalms. A vessel filled with water from the Pool of Shiloam was carried into the temple where it was received with a trumpet fanfare and the recitation of Isaiah 12:3 ("With joy you will draw water from the wells of salvation"). This water was mixed with sacrificial wine to the accompaniment of more music and was then poured out beside the altar—symbolizing its offering to God. The custom arose of illuminating the women's court of the temple on the evening of the next day with lamps that gave light to the whole city. Musicians standing on the court steps played instruments and sang, while prominent men and the priests performed a dance. The pageantry and spectacle made it into a popular festival that was even observed in synagogues far away from Jerusalem.[15]

The Day of Atonement (Lev 23:26–32) was the only fast day commanded in the Old Testament. All work was forbidden and the people gathered in a holy convocation. It was on this day that blood was brought into the holy of holies by the priest as the representative of the people to make atonement for the priests and then for the whole congregation of Israel. The ceremonies began with the priest's donning a simple white garment (suggesting purity). He then sacrificed a bull as a sin offering for himself and the priesthood, after which he entered the holy of holies to offer incense that produced a cloud over the mercy seat. Finally, he sprinkled the blood of the bull on the mercy seat and on the ground in front of the ark.

The rituals for making atonement for the people were distinct from these. A male goat was sacrificed and its blood was sprinkled in the same manner as the sin offering for the priests. After the purification of the holy place and the altar of burnt offerings with the mingled blood of the goat and bull, the priest took a second goat, laid his hands on its head, and confessed the sins of Israel, effectively "laying" those sins on the goat. This scapegoat (i.e., "escape goat") was then driven into the wilderness, symbolically

---

15. Gehman, "Tabernacles, Feast of," 921–22.

taking the people's sins with it, far away from the holy place. The remains of the two sacrificed animals were burned, and there was a concluding service. Following the destruction of the temple, only the traditions of fasting and refraining from work remained. A shofar (ram's horn trumpet) was sounded in order to summon people to an "All Vows" service, in which the people ask God to forgive their failure to keep their previous vows. A second service was held throughout the next day, and the observance concluded with another shofar blast to dismiss the people.[16]

Israel's key time observances need to be understood in light of our discussions about ritual and the life sciences in chapter 2. Like other aspects of ritual, Israel's sacred timekeeping was related to sacred story. As a celebration of the provision of food, the Feast of Weeks points back to God's promise to provide for the people he liberated from Egypt (Exod 3:8). The Passover/Unleavened Bread and Feast of Booths memorialized the exodus event, and with the rituals of these two feasts, the people "acted out" Israel's central story ("myth"), such that they came to "know" themselves as "God's chosen people."

The Feast of Booths can also be explained by way of cultural anthropology. Essentially, this celebration enabled Israel to return to an earlier state of its existence, namely, a people wandering in the Sinai wilderness. It was an opportunity for Israel to recapture that liminal existence in which it was no longer a slave people, but not yet a nation in possession of the promised land—a state in which it was entirely dependent on God. Every celebration of this feast afforded an experience of *communitas* since everyone lived in simple huts. By restoring a sense of dependence on God and providing a shared experience, the Feast of Booths renewed the community both in faith toward God and in mutual love. Ultimately, the Feast of Booths looked not only to what once was, but also to what Israel could be in its present and future as God's people.

We might relate the Day of Atonement to Asad and Mitchell's notion of a "technology for instilling virtue." While the ritual involvement of the people may have been minimal on this occasion, the visual effect would have been striking. The confession of Israel's sins over the animal and its expulsion into the wilderness undoubtedly impressed upon the assembly the need for truthfulness about human sin and the urge to suppress it. In symbolizing the need for Israel to "drive sin away," the scapegoat ritual

16. Pfeiffer, "Atonement, Day of," 104–5.

sought to instill the virtues of honesty and humility—both necessary for a life lived before a holy God.

Besides these annual feasts, sacred time in Israel included the weekly sabbath observance (Heb., *sabat*, "to cease") on the "seventh" day when the people of Israel rested in imitation of God's cessation from activity following the six days of creation (Exod 20:8). Thus, the sabbath remembered God's creative work and confessed his sovereignty over creation. But more than that, because the sabbath was blessed and hallowed by God, it allowed Israel to live out its identity as God's chosen people. At a practical level, the sabbath provided a needed respite for work animals and human laborers (Exod 23:12). The cessation of work also witnessed to God's act of delivering Israel from its oppressive labors in Egypt. So essential was the sabbath to Israel's identity and its relationship with God that violators were to be put to death (Num 15:32–36). Not surprisingly, the prophets condemned violations of the sabbath (Isa 56:2). Like other liturgical observances in Israel, the sabbath was to be marked by a sacred worship assembly of the people (Lev 23:3). During the Babylonian exile the study of the law (Torah) became a common sabbath activity.

Sabbath observance became a hallmark of universal Judaism between 400 BCE and the first century CE because of its scriptural basis, weekly observance, and its ability to be observed anywhere because of its association with time rather than location. The one challenge, of course, was the ongoing need to define what exactly constituted work, e.g., whether one could in engage in military battle on the sabbath. Circumcision was permitted and the necessity of preserving life took precedence over sabbath regulations.[17]

The day itself had appointed times for prayer. Psalm 55 (v. 17) indicates that individuals prayed in the morning, at noon, and in the evening. Psalm 141:2 speaks of the last of these prayer times as the worshipper's "evening sacrifice." The morning and evening prayer times became a memorial of the daily sacrifices offered in the temple at these times.[18]

Less common in Israel's experience but no less important were the Sabbatical and Jubilee Years. The Sabbatical Year brought a complete rest for the land: after six years of normal agricultural activity, there was to be no sowing or gathering of crops (Lev 25:2). Essentially, the land was left fallow in order

---

17. See Jesus' discourse on the Sabbath in Matthew 12:11–12, where he speaks of saving an imperiled animal on the Sabbath, an action that was deemed acceptable.

18. Bradshaw, "Daily Prayer," 141.

to restore its fertility and to avoid overproduction and wastage. What nevertheless grew was left for the poor to gather or for wild animals to consume (Exod 23:11). The period was dedicated to the Lord, in recognition that the land was a gift from God and thus needed to be cared for by the people.[19] Additionally, the end of the Sabbatical Year brought the cancellation of all debts (Deut 15:2–8) as a means of poverty alleviation (v. 4).

Following seven Sabbaticals (i.e., the forty-ninth year), the fiftieth year was to be observed as the Jubilee (Lev 25:8–12).[20] The event was heralded by the blowing of a ram's horn (Heb., *yobel*), from which the observance derived its name. It included all of the prohibitions of the normal Sabbatical Year, plus the reversion of property to the original owners and the liberation of slaves. The Jubilee Year served to express thanks to God who gave the land to humanity, which implied both that no human was the sole owner of any land and could not own it forever. Like the Sabbatical Year, the Jubilee Year was grounded in the belief that Israel did not inherently possess the land but had received it as a gift from God (Deut 15:4–5). Similarly, the practice of freeing slaves was done in recognition that the Israelites themselves had been freed from slavery by God (Deut 15:15). Because there is insufficient historical evidence to support its actual observance, the Jubilee was most likely no more than an ideal, expressive of Israel's social values.[21]

Neither historical nor agricultural in nature, the *new moon* was observed to mark the beginning of the month, since the Jewish calendar was lunar. It was a holy day with additional sacrifices (Num 28:11–15), the blowing of a trumpet (Num 10:10; Ps 81:3), and the cessation of work (Amos 8:5). It was generally a joyful occasion (1 Sam 20:5). The new moon of the seventh month was considered especially sacred and was accordingly observed as a sabbath, with a public worship gathering (Lev 23:23–24).

19. Freeman, "Sabbatical Year," 1033.

20. Freeman, "Sabbatical Year," 1033. Because the Jubilee Year occurred immediately after a regular Sabbatical Year, there would have been two successive years without any harvesting, which raises the possibility of food shortages. To respond to this problem, God gave Israel the assurance that the sixth year would provide enough food for three successive years, that is, enough to get through the Jubilee Year (Lev 25:20–22).

21. Freeman, "Sabbatical Year," 1033; Gehman, "Jubilee," 521–22.

Non-Pentateuchal Festivals

Thus far we have considered those observances whose origins and regulatory materials are found in the Pentateuch. But a number of festivals observed in ancient Israel have their origins in scriptural material outside of the Pentateuch.

Purim (Heb., the lot used for determining a question by chance) is observed on the fourteenth and fifteenth days of Adar in the Jewish calendar to commemorate the deliverance of the Jews from the genocidal plot of Haman during the time of Queen Esther (9:21–28). The observance, known by the ancient historian of the Jews, Josephus, was celebrated throughout the land, and not just in Jerusalem, meaning that it was not a pilgrimage festival like Passover or the Feast of Weeks. Its ritual actions witness to its focus on historical remembrance. The day of 13 Adar involved a fast to prepare the body and mind for focusing on the sacred events to be commemorated. On the evening of that day (i.e., the beginning of 14 Adar), communities of Jews assembled in synagogues and listened to the reading of the book of Esther, verbalizing curses against Haman at the mention of his name. Worship continued the next morning with another service in the synagogue, and the remainder of the day was given to celebrating and rejoicing.[22] It has been customary in some Jewish communities for wealthier members to give alms to the poor on Purim. Thus, rejoicing in God's grace-filled deliverance of the people and reflecting that grace through acts of charity are central to the observance of Purim.

Hanukkah (Heb., "dedication") was instituted by the Jewish patriot Judas Maccabeus (190–160 BCE) to commemorate the rededication of the Jerusalem temple after its desecration by the Seleucid ruler Antiochus IV Epiphanes (1 Macc 4:41–59). The celebration encompassed eight days starting with the twenty-fifth day of the month of Chislem (i.e., early/mid-December). The history of the event begins with the looting of the Second Temple in Jerusalem and cessation of services due to the conquest of the city by Antiochus IV Epiphanies. This prompted a revolt led by the priest Matthias, which finally succeeded under Judas Maccabeus, who liberated the temple and saw to its rededication. Miraculously, a four-day supply of oil for the sacred lamps lasted eight days, hence the length of the observance.[23] Traditionally, Hanukkah is observed with rejoicing

---

22. Freeman, "Purim," 991; Gehman, "Purim," 782.

23. Gehman, "Feast," 296.

and thanksgiving, fasting being deemed inappropriate. Today, candles are lighted on an eight-branch candelabra (menorah), with the number of candles lighted being progressively increased until the eighth day. The celebrations are entirely domestic in character and usually involve gift exchanges and the eating of special foods, especially fried fare to recall the original oil miracle in the temple. Thus, like other Jewish festivals, Hanukkah serves the purpose of historical remembrance and group identity formation within the Jewish community.

Life Cycle Rituals in the Old Testament

Circumcision

Human communities have long had rituals for initiating persons into their society, and in the case of Israel this is circumcision—the surgical removal of the foreskin of a male's penis. Instituted by God, it was to be a sign of God's covenant with Abraham, who was to circumcise himself, his male children, and his slaves (Gen. 17:1–10, 21). The eighth day after birth was identified as the proper time for circumcision, but those born after the promulgation of the ordinance could undergo the procedures at any age. Scholars speculate that circumcision was originally a puberty rite that was transferred to infancy, perhaps because it was easier and more convenient to carry out circumcision on babies, as opposed to young adolescents.[24] The biblical evidence suggests that circumcision is a means of establishing identity, since all foreigners who wished to join the community of Israel were required to undergo the rite (Exod 12:48–49). The "uncircumcised," a derogatory term, became synonymous with Gentiles or those outside of Israel, since many non-Israelite peoples, such as the Philistines, did not practice circumcision (1 Sam 17:26).

But why ritualize initiation with a procedure that is risky, bloody, and painful? Here it is important to understand the connection between circumcision and obedience. Those who were members of the covenant community had to live in constant obedience to God's laws, and this idea is mentioned throughout the Bible (e.g., Jer 4:4; Rom 2:25–29). To some extent, circumcision suggests the idea of consecration to God, but this is much less important than the idea of being marked as a member of the covenant community. Rather than suggestive of the costliness of

24. Gehman, "Circumcision," 176–77.

obedience, the blood shed in circumcision signifies the "costly demand which God makes of those whom he calls to himself and marks with the sign of his covenant."[25]

Marriage

Because marriage was a domestic matter involving two families, the Old Testament does not contain ritual prescriptions for marriage. Rather, it offers scattered glimpses of ancient nuptial practices. The process began when a young man's parents selected a spouse for him and undertook negotiations with the prospective bride's family. In some cases, the woman may have been asked to give her consent (Gen 24:58). After successful negotiations, there was an official betrothal or pledge to marry, which obligated both parties to carry through on the promises. Any publicizing of the marriage was done entirely at the initiative of the future groom. To seal the covenant and bind the families together, the man gave a gift to the woman's family, and the father of the bride presented a dowry gift to the bride and her husband, e.g., household servants (Gen 24:59). The man gave his bride jewels and/or clothing (Gen 24:53).

On the wedding day itself, the bride bedecked herself in jewels (Isa 61:10), a girdle (Jer 2:32), and a veil (Gen 24:65). Besides wearing his best clothing, the groom may have worn a garland (Isa 61:10). Only royal brides had bridesmaids, but all grooms had a group of companions. The party of men journeyed to the house of the bride, where festivities may have already begun. The groom and his companions then escorted the bride back to the groom's home or to the home of his father (Ps 45:14), amid singing and dancing illumined by lamps if at nighttime (Jer 7:34). A feast was held at the groom's home, usually at night, with attendees wearing festive clothing. At some point the groom would have covered the bride with the skirt of his clothing to symbolize his protection of her (Ruth 3:9). Parents and friends offered a blessing and well-wishes (Gen 24:60). The couple was escorted by their parents to an especially prepared bridechamber where the marriage was to be consummated (Ps 19:5; Joel 2:16). A blood-stained cloth was displayed in order to prove the bride's virginity (Deut 22:13–21). Festivities could continue long afterwards, perhaps even weeks. But not all of these activities were necessarily included in every marriage.[26]

25. Motyer, "Circumcision," 205.
26. Wright and Thompson, "Marriage," 733–34.

The marital practices described above constitute a rite of passage. The movement of the group to the home of the bride and then the procession of bride and groom back to the groom's home symbolize the journey inherent in marriage: from childhood to adulthood, from life as single persons to that of a married couple. The feast not only ritualizes social approval of the marriage, but also honors bride and groom in their new identity as husband and wife. They are welcomed into their new social statuses, and the bride is welcomed into a new family. Although domestic in character, marriage nevertheless captured the imagination of prophets like Isaiah and Jeremiah, suggesting the degree to which the practices were part of the psyche of ancient people.

Consecrations: Priests, Kings, and Prophets

Given that the priests of the old covenant served as mediators between the Israelite community and God through sacrifices and other acts, it is not surprising that they were set apart for their duties by means of special rituals of consecration. According to the first set of instructions in Exodus 29, Aaron and his sons were to be brought to the tent of meeting where they were washed. They were then dressed in the priestly garments, including a special turban. Aaron was then anointed with oil that was poured over this head. Then followed a sin offering of a bull whose flesh and internal organs were burnt while the hide and intestines were hidden outside the camp. Next a ram was burnt up as an act of appeasement to the Lord. Another ram ("the ram for the ordination") was then sacrificed, and Aaron and his sons made a wave offering using a loaf of unleavened bread, which is then burned on the altar along with parts of the ordination ram. The breast of the ram is waved as an offering to the Lord, and then consecrated along with the thigh meat. The latter serves as an offering of the people on behalf of Aaron and his sons, who eat the meat at the entrance of the tent of meeting, along with the aforementioned bread. This particular offering is so sacred that it can only be consumed by the consecrated priests and any meat that remains until the following morning must be burned. Following these actions, the event continues for seven days with daily bull sacrifices that serve to make atonement for the altar, which is also anointed with oil.[27] Details

---

27. No reason is given as to why the altar needs to have atonement made for it. Perhaps there was a perception that contact with human hands had defiled it. Interestingly, after this purification of the altar, whatever touched it became holy.

added by the second account of the priestly ordination (Lev 8:1–36) include the presidency of Moses over the proceedings, the placement of the Urim and Thummim[28] in the breast piece of Aaron's vestments, the anointing of the tabernacle, the splashing of blood on the altar, the placement of animal blood on the right ears and big toes of Aaron and his sons, the consecration of the priests and their vestments with both oil and blood from the altar, and the command for Aaron and his sons to remain at the entrance to the tent of meeting for seven days and seven nights.

Insofar as prophets spoke authoritatively on God's behalf to the people of Israel, and received their message through the Holy Spirit's inspiration (2 Chr 24:20), we might have expected them to be consecrated with divinely appointed rituals, especially anointing. However, textual evidence for prophetical anointing is lacking. While Elijah was "directed" by God to anoint his successor, Elisha (1 Kgs 19:16), there is no explicit indication in the Elijah-Elisha narratives that this actually occurred. It may well be that the former's action of placing his cloak around the latter (19:19) served as the necessary consecration. Other biblical passages suggestive of a prophetic anointing need not be read as such. Psalm 105:15 ("Do not touch my [God's] anointed ones! Do no harm to my prophets!") actually references the patriarchs, rather than prophets. Isaiah 61:1 ("The Spirit of the Lord God is on me, because the Lord has anointed me to preach good news to the poor") is probably not referring to a literal anointing at all, but to a metaphorical one.

But if they were not ritually anointed, were prophets antithetical to ritual in ancient Israel? It is tempting to answer "no" based on the perception that prophets were inherent fixtures of shrines and temples just as priests were. However, while prophets and prophetic groups may have ministered at such places, it would be inaccurate to speak of "cultic prophets" and "cultic prophetic guilds," due to a lack of sufficient evidence on the matter.[29] Nevertheless, prophets were not necessarily anti-ritualistic in their outlook. In a number of passages where prophets criticize the worship of the people, worship itself is not really the main target. When Jeremiah condemns all those entering the temple (ch. 7), it is not because they engage in forbidden rituals, but rather because they show little concern for pursuing lives of righteousness (7:3, 5–6, 9) and seem to think that their wickedness can escape judgment because they were in the very house

---

28. Special objects used for divination by the priests.

29. Motyer, "Prophecy, Prophets," 970.

where God's name dwells (v. 10). Although Amos speaks of God spurning the sacrifices of the people (5:21–23), the rejection is due to the people's lack of morality and holiness. Thus, the real problem for Amos is a disconnection between spirituality and morality. A similar argument could be made about Micah 6:6–8, which seems to denigrate or downplay temple sacrifice but stresses the morality of the people. Finally, we should note that in Isaiah 43:22–25, God denounces the *neglect* of sacrificial worship and promises the rebuilding of the temple (44:28), all of which amounts to an affirmation of Israel's sacrificial worship.

While the evidence for prophetic anointing is sparse, kings in the Old Testament clearly were consecrated through a ritual anointing. Among those kings anointed were the following: Saul (1 Sam 9:16; 10:1), David (1 Sam 16:1, 12–13), Solomon (1 Kgs 1:34), Joash (2 Kgs 11:12), and Jehu (1 Kgs 19:16). The officiant was either a priest (e.g., Zadok in the case of Solomon, and Jehoiada in the case of Joash), or a prophet (Samuel in the cases of Saul and David, and Elijah in the case Jehu). The oil was poured on the king's head from either a flask or a horn. While anointing seems to be the original ritual used for designating early kings, other rituals were added over time, e.g., crowning, a formal proclamation (2 Kgs 11:12), and seating the king on a throne (2 Kgs 11:19). The ceremony would have been accompanied by sacrifices, and often included a procession (1 Kgs 1:9; 1:40). Together these ritual actions served to identify a particular person with the office of king in order to invite the respect and loyalty of the people. The administration of the anointing by a priest or prophet pointed to the king's divine calling to dispense justice and righteousness (Ps 72:1–2), which was particularly important given Israel's identity as a people rescued from slavery.

Funerals

As with marriage, the ritualization of death and entombment in ancient Israel was domestic in character and did not involve an official liturgy conducted by religious specialists. Descriptions of death rituals are scattered throughout the literature of the Old Testament. Death occasioned loud mourning and lamentation by family members (Gen 50:10), usually at the home of the deceased where professional mourners could be employed (Jer 9:17). The time of mourning often extended to seven days (Gen 50:10; Ezek 3:15). Today we would say that the practices of intentional mourning were about permission-giving. The presence of professional (and other) mourners was a sign that mourning was socially acceptable, and allowing an extended period for mourning was a way for the community to give the bereaved social and emotional space for accepting the death of a family member and thus making the transition to life without this person's presence.

Mourners engaged in any number of ritualistic practices, including rending their garments (2 Sam 1:11, 13:31), wearing sackcloth (Joel 1:8), scattering dust on themselves, and sitting in ashes (Jer 6:26). We might note that these are also rituals associated with repentance—the mourning over one's sins or the sins of others. The body is made unattractive through rough clothing and dirt to image death and the ugliness of human sin in God's sight. Ultimately, these rituals point to humanity's need for redemption from sin and death by the God who created the body.

The narrative of Sarah's death in Genesis 23 indicates that burial took place soon after death in a location away from human settlements, due to the rapid decomposition of corpses in the Near Eastern climate. Generally, cremation was not practiced by the ancient Jewish people. Spices or burned aromatics might be added to the body (Jer 34:5), which was carried on a bier (2 Sam 3:31) to the place of burial, normally a horizontally carved chamber in a rocky cliff (Gen 25:9–10). Usually family members were entombed in proximity to one another.[30]

Ritual in the New Testament

Baptism

Just as ancient Israel "initiated" male children through circumcision, so the early church initiated people into its ranks through baptism. Serving as precursors to Christian baptism are the purifying washings of the Essene community and John's "baptism of repentance for the forgiveness of sins" (Mark 1:4). By submitting to John's baptism, a person acknowledged himself to be a sinner in need of salvation from God's wrath. According to John, the coming savior would baptize with the Holy Spirit and fire (Matt 3:11). The relationship between Jesus and the Holy Spirit becomes apparent in his own baptism by John, which is accompanied by the Holy Spirit's

---

30. Gehman, "Burial," 129; Gehman, "Mourning," 640; Gehman, "Sepulcher," 848–49; Kitchen, "Burial and Mourning," 149–50.

descent on Jesus in the form of a dove (Matt 3:16–17). In light of the biblical significance of the Holy Spirit, we can say that Jesus' baptism implies two things: (1) he is the Spirit-endowed servant of God sent to bring justice to the world (Isa 42:1), and (2) the eschatological day of deliverance had dawned with the promised outpouring of God's Spirit on his servants (Joel 2:28–29). Thus, Jesus is initiated into his ministry by way of baptism.

Striking are the references in John's gospel to Jesus' own acts of baptizing. Twice the evangelist reports that Jesus baptized (3:22; 4:1), only to state subsequently that it was not Jesus who baptized in Judea, but rather his disciples (4:2). It may be that this gloss represents a certain discomfort with the idea of Jesus baptizing, since it suggests that his ministry bore similarities to John's. Indeed, it has been suggested that the tradition about Jesus administering baptism was either forgotten or deliberately ignored in order to avoid subordinating Jesus to John. But if Jesus did indeed baptize, it would make the lines of ritual continuity clearer: the baptism administered by John was received by Jesus, who himself baptized and commanded his disciples to baptize, which they did in obedience to that command.[31] Thus the church today baptizes both to obey Jesus' command and to follow his example.

The connection between the church's baptism and Jesus is seen in the so-called "Great Commission":

> Then Jesus came to them and said, "All authority in heaven and on earth has been given to Me. Therefore, go and make disciples of all nations, baptizing them in the name of the Father, and of the Son, and of the Holy Spirit, and teaching them to obey all that I have commanded you. And surely, I am with you always, even to the end of the age." (Matt 28:18–20)

This text has been understood as Jesus' official sanction of baptism as the church's rite of initiation. The language of "Father, Son and Holy Spirit"—perhaps more reflective of the theology of the early church than that of the historical Jesus—suggests that those who receive baptism are brought into a special relationship with Jesus, the Son of God, the Father who sent Jesus, and the Spirit whom the Father sends on Jesus and his followers. What in fact makes Christian baptism distinct is the promise that it will impart the Holy Spirit who gives new birth (John 3:5; Titus 3:5), and empowers Jesus' followers to share his story with the world (Acts 1:8).

31. See Collins, "Origin of Christian Baptism," 48–49. Cited in Johnson, ed., *Rites of Christian Initiation*, 19.

That the earliest followers of Jesus viewed baptism as central to their missionary endeavors is clear from the book of Acts. On the day of Pentecost, the apostle Peter enjoins his hearers to receive baptism that they might have their sins forgiven and receive the Holy Spirit (2:38). In response, a throng of three thousand persons received baptism, which was surely administered by the apostles themselves. Later, the apostle Philip baptizes people in Samaria (8:12) and an Ethiopian (Acts 8:38). Paul, the apostle to the non-Jewish world, was baptized following his Damascus road experience (9:18), and he himself baptized others (16:33; cf. 1 Cor 1:14–16). In two cases in Acts, baptisms apparently deemed deficient were supplemented with an apostolic laying on of hands for the impartation of the Holy Spirit (8:15–17; 19:1–7). But it is unclear whether a ritual hand-laying was considered as normative for baptism in the primitive church.

The New Testament offers few ritual details about baptism. Accounts in Acts (2:41, 8:38) indicate that Jesus' apostles were the earliest ministers of baptism. Paul speaks of his own baptismal activity (1 Cor 1:16), but notes that this was not a central feature of his ministry. Adults able to speak for themselves were the normal recipients of baptism, although the baptism of "households" (Acts 16:15, 33; 1 Cor 1:16) raises the possibility that children received baptism in the first century. (The first sure evidence for the baptism of children only emerges in the late second century/early third century.) In any event, the New Testament does not explicitly forbid the baptism of infants and young children.

Also lacking is any indication of how water was applied at baptism, whether by sprinkling, pouring, or immersing. On this matter we have to rely on ancient artistic depictions of baptism, some of which show a candidate standing in waist-deep water, while other iconography depicts the candidate standing in ankle-deep water.[32] The former artworks hint of baptismal immersion, while the latter would suggest pouring/affusion. The baptisms of Jesus and the Ethiopian indicate settings in natural bodies of water, but the New Testament does not mandate an outdoor setting for baptism. As for the words spoken during the administration of baptism, i.e., the baptismal formula, we only find possibilities in Matthew 28:19 ("in the name of the Father, and of the Son, and of the Holy Spirit") and Acts 8:16 ("in

---

32. According to Robin Jensen, the small, childlike figure in ankle-deep water being baptized by John is a dual depiction of Jesus and the ordinary Christian baptismal candidate. The linkage with Jesus suggests that Jesus' baptism is a prototype for Christian baptism, while the child figure implies that baptism returns one to a state of childlike innocence brought about by the forgiveness of sins. Jensen, *Baptismal Imagery*, 16.

the name of Jesus"). Since these phraseologies are not explicitly prescribed for liturgical use, we cannot know for certain whether they represent actual liturgical formulae. Some scholars have suggested that they may be no more than theological interpretations of the meaning of baptism.[33]

Rather than providing ritual details about baptism, the New Testament as a whole is mostly concerned about the meaning of baptism. Basically, baptism ritualizes one's acceptance of the apostolic message about Jesus and his resurrection (Acts 2:38) and one's inclusion into a Christian community. The New Testament also offers several interpretative images that depict baptism as: (1) the reception of the Holy Spirit (Acts 2:38); (2) death and resurrection with Jesus (Rom 6:1–4; Col 2:12); (3) being clothed with Christ (Gal 3:27); and (4) regeneration with/in the Holy Spirit (John 3:5; Titus 3:5). In addition, if Jesus' own baptism is paradigmatic for Christian baptism, then baptism represents one's adoption as God's beloved son or daughter who is empowered by the Holy Spirit for doing God's work in the world. Finally, Ephesians 4:5 indicates that baptism is a sign of church unity, along with one faith, one Lord Jesus, and "one God and Father of us all." This discussion would suggest that baptism, like other rituals, cannot be limited to meaning only one thing, and that additional ritual gestures (e.g., anointing, clothing with a new garment, the presentation of a lighted candle) are needed to bring out the full meaning of baptism.

But why is a bath the central ritual in Christian initiation? The answer has to do with the fact that bathing and washing are human universals that naturally take on symbolic significance. Specifically, washing and bathing represent cleansing, purity, renewal, and rebirth. Given that repentance—the acceptance of one's sinfulness and desire for redemption—is central to Christian initiation (Acts 2:38), and given that sin is identified with uncleanness in the Bible (Lev 16:16; Isa 1:16), washing/bathing most aptly portrays what the transition into the Christian faith means. The reception of baptism demonstrates that one has been cleansed of an old self and has become a new person with a new faith in a new community.

The Lord's Supper in the New Testament

The names commonly used for the Lord's Supper are all derived from the New Testament. "Lord's Supper" itself is used by Paul in 1 Corinthians 11:20, and serves to underscore not only the origin of the meal in Jesus

33. Johnson, *Rites of Christian Initiation*, 35.

himself, but also suggests his very presence in that meal. "Holy Communion" references 1 Corinthians 10:16, where Paul states that the bread and cup of the meal offer participation (Gk., *koinonia*, communion) in the body and blood of the Lord. In other words, to eat the bread and drink from the cup of the Lord's Supper is to experience intimate fellowship with the Lord Jesus. "Eucharist" derives from the Greek verb meaning "to give thanks" as the Lord Jesus did over the bread and cup at the Last Supper (Luke 22:19). In using this particular term for the Supper, we emphasize the act of prayerfully thanking God for his benefits bestowed both in history and in the bread and cup before us. Less common nomenclature for the Supper includes terms such as "Sacrament of the Altar" and "Sacrament of the Table," which highlight the sacredness of the event, that is, the presence of God that is manifested.

Christians believe that the Lord's Supper is a tradition given by the Lord Jesus himself. The first three gospels all contain accounts of the meal that Jesus had with his disciples on the evening of his betrayal (Matt 26:26–29; Mark 14:22–25; Luke 22:15–20), with a fourth account provided by Paul in 1 Corinthians 11 (vv. 23–26). While the versions in Matthew and Mark are similar, those of Luke and Paul align. The basic difference between these two sets involves whether the cup action takes place during the meal, as in Matthew and Mark, or after it, as in Luke and Paul.

What is described in the "words of institution" closely follows the ritual pattern of the Jewish sacred meal, in which the head of the household took bread, prayed in thanksgiving, broke and then shared the bread with the other participants, and, following the completion of the meal, took a cup of wine, offered a longer prayer, and then shared it with his companions. Insofar as it includes Jesus' command to "do this in memory of me" (or in some translations "do this for the remembrance of me"), the institution narrative in the gospels and 1 Corinthians has served as a warrant for Christians to celebrate the meal perpetually. "Remembering/ remembrance" reflects a Greek word (*anamnesis*) whose rich meaning suggests that the event being remembered is a present reality with all its saving benefits for God's people. Thus, to share a meal that remembers Jesus is to experience the very presence of God's messiah, who brings both the judgment and salvation of the final days.

The meaning of the Lord's Supper ritual draws on the various Old Testament sacrifices. The synoptic gospels of Matthew, Mark, and Luke indicate that Jesus' final meal with his disciples was a Passover supper.

Like the Passover, the Christian Supper remembers a saving event and ritual participation occurs through the eating of the sacrificial victim. Like the peace/fellowship offerings, the Lord's Supper includes the giving of thanks for a benefit received, namely, Jesus, in whose presence the participants eat and drink ("this is my body," "this cup is the new covenant in my blood"). Finally, atonement, central to the meaning of the guilt and sin offerings of the Old Testament, finds expression in the Lord's Supper in that the cup offers the blood that was shed "for the forgiveness of sins." Thus, the Lord's Supper draws together old sacrificial themes so as to interpret the meal in relation to the life, death, and resurrection of Jesus, who himself is manifested in the meal.

Jesus' presence in the meal had important ritual implications for Paul and his relationship with the Corinthian church. To him it appeared that the Lord's Supper in Corinth involved separate meals for the wealthy members versus poorer ones who arrived later only to receive no food at all. For Paul the "private meals" (11:21) of wealthy members brought about a fracturing of the community and a subversion of the meal's meaning as participation in the Lord, whose saving work united people into one community (1 Cor 10:17; Gal 3:28; Eph 2:14). (Here we should note that in the case of the Corinthian church, the actions with bread and cup were part of a full fellowship meal.) Paul's point in 1 Corinthians 11 is clear: the Supper cannot accentuate social differences and create divisions within the church; to do so is to desecrate the meal and sin against the very body of the Lord (v. 27).

Other than the ritual sequence of taking bread, giving thanks, and sharing it, and similarly with the cup, the New Testament offers few ritual details about the actual celebration of the Lord's Supper. As for leadership of the meal, the Supper was, in a sense, "given" to the twelve disciples, those chosen by Jesus for carrying on his ministry in the world. Thus, the church has understood that the prerogative for leadership at the Supper lies with those chosen by the church for such leadership. That the meal or "breaking of bread" was subject to apostolic presidency is suggested by Acts 2:42, 20:11, and 27:35.[34] There is no mention in the New Testament about the proper recipients of the Supper, and other than Paul's prescription for self-examination in 1 Corinthians 11:28–29, there is no material about how to prepare for participation in the Supper. However, given that Luke's reference to the Lord's Supper in the Jerusalem church follows a note about three

34. "Breaking of bread" is Luke's technical term for celebrating the Lord's Supper.

thousand people being baptized, it would not be unreasonable to conclude that participation in the Supper was reserved for the baptized. Since it regards baptism as a mark of Christian identity, the New Testament can hardly be interpreted as sanctioning communion for unbaptized persons.

Similarly, there are few details about the timing of the Lord's Supper. The first three gospels indicate that Jesus' evening meal with the disciples was a celebration of the Passover meal (Matt 26:17; Mark 14:12; Luke 22:1), while the fourth gospel locates this meal prior to the day of Passover (John 13:1). But Christians have never limited the Supper to a once-a-year celebration coinciding with the Jewish Passover. However, they have marked Thursday in Holy Week with a celebration of the Lord's Supper, since the Supper was instituted three days before the Lord's resurrection. If the Lord's Supper has a connection with any day, it would be Sunday, the first day of the week. On the evening of the day of Jesus' resurrection, two disciples encounter the risen Lord, who is made known to them "in the breaking of the bread" (Luke 24:13–35). In Acts 20:7 Paul breaks bread with Christians in Troas on the first day—although it is not clear whether "evening of the first day" refers to sundown on a Saturday or to a Sunday evening. If the latter, the meal would technically not have occurred on a Sunday at all, but at the beginning of a Monday according to the biblical understanding of when the new day begins.[35]

As for the food and beverage used by Jesus, there can be no doubt that he used wine, since the ancient world knew of no unfermented grape drink and lacked the technology for producing and maintaining such. If the Last Supper and the Lord's passion occurred in the spring season (i.e., at the time of the Passover), only a fermented beverage could have endured the storage period between its production in the late summer months to its consumption in the spring of the year. Red wine was likely used, since white varieties of grapes were uncommon in the ancient Near East. For many Christians, the red color of the wine has come to symbolize Christ's blood, but that connection is not made explicit in the New Testament. Most likely the bread used at the Last Supper was unleavened bread, since it was easier to make and less expensive than leavened bread.[36] But even if that were the case, there is no biblical prescription concerning the type of bread to be used; only the Passover context of the passion narrative can serve as a reason for using unleavened bread in services of Holy Communion.

35. Genesis 1:8 suggests that the day begins at sundown.

36. McGowan, *Ancient Christian Worship*, 22.

Like bathing, gathering for a meal and eating is a human universal. Because of that, eating carries strong symbolic significance. A meal symbolizes fellowship and community with others, as well as joy and celebration. Performance theory teaches us that a meal brings these things into effect. Since Christian life involves a personal union with the risen Lord Jesus and membership in a community of fellow believers, a ritual meal is a fitting way of maintaining these relationships. It is unfortunate, however, when the supper is celebrated as a somber memorial of Christ's death such that it lacks the joy of communing with the risen Lord who triumphed over death. Equally lamentable is the shrinkage of the bread and cup to a mere sip of wine/juice and the consumption of small wafers that bear little resemblance to actual bread. Gone here is the sense of actually eating and drinking in the presence of a living Savior. Any "revival" of the Lord's Supper and renewal of its significance for the church will require a consideration of what exactly a meal means and brings into existence through its ritual performance.

The Liturgical Calendar and the New Testament

The strongest evidence in the New Testament for the ritual observance of a particular day of devotion is for Sunday, the first day of the week. All of the gospels report that Jesus was raised on this day following his crucifixion and entombment. While it offers no prescriptions for observing Sunday in order to memorialize the Lord's resurrection, the New Testament does hint that Sunday was a day to gather for preaching/instruction and the celebration of the Lord's Supper. According to Luke 24:13–35, two disciples met the risen Lord on the afternoon/early evening of the day of his resurrection (Sunday), and were instructed by him concerning what is said of him in the (Old Testament) Scriptures. Later, Jesus shares a meal in which he is made known to them "in the breaking of the bread." It has been suggested that this passage serves to express the meaning of the Sunday worship assembly, namely, that it is an encounter with the risen Lord through the reading of the Scriptures and the sharing of the sacramental meal.[37] According to Acts 20:7 Paul met with a group of Christians on the evening of first day of the week to "break bread" and to speak to them (i.e., preach)—although we cannot be certain whether this is a reference to a Saturday or a Sunday evening.

37. Lathrop, *Holy Things*, 48–49.

Elsewhere in the New Testament, there are references to Sunday that may or may not have anything to do with Christian worship practices. Paul instructs Christians in Corinth to set aside money for a collection on the first day (1 Cor 16:2), but it is not clear whether any kind of worship gathering is in view here. Additionally, in Revelation 1:10 the seer speaks of being "in the spirit on the Lord's Day"—a term that will come to be used for Sunday. However, this text does not specifically mention a worship gathering. It should also be noted that "Lord's Day" may not even be a reference to Sunday at all, but rather to the eschatological day of the Lord when Jesus returns in glory.

If nothing else, the annual cycle of Old Testament liturgical festivals is well known to New Testament authors and their respective Christian communities. Jesus' supper with his disciples on the night of his betrayal is identified as a Passover meal by the Synoptic Gospels, while John's Gospel indicates that this repast occurred prior to the Passover. The association of the Lord's Supper and Passover suggests that by eating the bread and drinking the wine identified with Jesus' body and blood, Christians participate in a new saving event that takes its meaning from Jesus' sacrifice on the cross.

The Passover is also mentioned several times in John's Gospel, all in connection with significant events in Jesus' ministry: (1) the cleansing of the temple (2:13, 23); (2) the feeding of the multitude (6:4); and (3) Jesus' final week of earthly life, which culminates in his crucifixion. Viewed through the lens of the Passover, these three events point in some way to Jesus' role as the new sacrificial lamb (1:29): in the purification of the temple, the old sacrificial cult is driven away because Jesus is the new sacrificial victim who takes away sins; the feeding of the multitude at the hands of Jesus suggests that he himself, the new Passover lamb, is a source of food for God's people; the slaughtering of the new sacrificial Lamb takes place not in the temple, but on the cross.

The New Testament epistles contain only two references to the Passover. First, Paul refers to "Christ our Passover Lamb" (1 Cor 5:7–8) in an exhortation to do away with old sinful lives. Since Christ has been sacrificed for humanity's sins, believers should observe the new Passover by abstaining from the "old leavened bread of malice and wickedness" and by partaking of the "unleavened bread of sincerity and truth." Paul's injunction to observe the feast is metaphorical rather than literal, and most likely he assumed his audience's familiarity with the Passover. Second, Hebrews 11:28 states that Moses' observance of the original Passover was an act of faith in line with those of other biblical figures who trusted God and yet did not see the fulfillment of God's promises (vv. 39–40). Neither 1 Corinthians 5 nor Hebrews 11 commends the observance of Passover to Christians.

Besides Passover, Pentecost is also mentioned in the New Testament. According to Acts 2, the Holy Spirit was given to the disciples in Jerusalem on the day of Pentecost, which is Luke's term for the Jewish Feast of Weeks that occurs fifty days (Gk., *pentecostes*) after the Passover. Whether the coming of the Holy Spirit relates to any Jewish understanding of Pentecost/the Feast of Weeks is questionable. Prior to the emergence of Christianity, the fiftieth day after the Sabbath following the Passover was used to commemorate the giving of the law to Moses on Mt. Sinai—but most of the texts that make this connection emerge well after the appearance of Luke's Gospel. In the late first century, Pentecost was associated with covenant renewal. The association of the Spirit's outpouring on the disciples with the Jewish Feast of Weeks is probably no more than a way of explaining the presence of large numbers of people in Jerusalem.[38] While Jewish understandings may be absent, it is clear that the event marks the beginning of the church's mission to the world, with its focus on proclaiming Jesus as Lord and Messiah and calling people to repentance and baptism (Acts 2:38).

Elsewhere we find two other references to the day of Pentecost in the New Testament, namely, in Luke's note about Paul going with haste to Jerusalem (Acts 20:16), and Paul's own reference to staying at Ephesus until Pentecost (1 Cor 16:8). In both cases, Pentecost serves as no more than a time marker, for neither Luke nor Paul offer any comment about the significance of the feast day. Here again, of course, references to Pentecost suggest that the audiences of Paul and Luke had familiarity with the Jewish feast either through liturgical practice or by general knowledge. At the very least, we can detect no hostility on the part of Luke or Paul toward Pentecost in particular or toward the observance of sacred days in general.

The only reference to the Feast of Booths in the New Testament occurs in John 7, where Jesus makes his way to Jerusalem to begin teaching in the temple courts. On the last (eighth) day of the feast, which included an extrabiblical water ceremony meant to highlight the necessity of rain for watering crops, Jesus invites his hearers to come to him and drink (v. 37) that they might find living waters (Isa 12:3; 35:6). For Jesus, the Feast of Booths afforded an opportunity to proclaim himself a source of life and sustenance.

38. Gaventa, *Acts of the Apostles*, 74.

Finally, the Day of Atonement appears only as background to Hebrews chapters 9 and 10, where the author seeks to explain the preeminence of Jesus' sacrifice over Old Testament temple sacrifices. Jesus, he says, did not enter a humanly made tabernacle to make atonement year after year (proof of the inferiority of the old sacrifices), but entered heaven itself (9:24). Nor did he bring animal blood but offered his own blood, not only for outward ceremonial cleansing, but for the inward cleansing of the conscience (9:11–14). Additionally, Jesus suffered only "once for all" to take away the sins of many (9:26–27). The author concludes that the Day of Atonement sacrifices offer "only a shadow" (i.e., a type) of what would come in Jesus and, because they need to be repeated perpetually, these sacrifices are unable to atone for sin (10:1–4). By contrast, Jesus has performed the perfect sacrifice and has thereby cleansed people from their guilt. Accordingly, Jesus has brought an end to sacrifice (10:18) and has become the new high priest who has opened the way to heaven itself for all believers (10:20). This theology of the atoning work of Jesus explains why animal sacrifice was never part of Christian worship and why Protestants have rejected the idea that there is a Christian "priesthood" that offers the "sacrifice" of the mass.

Having considered the place of Jewish feasts in the New Testament, we might wonder about the New Testament grounding of the central Christian feasts that witness to the new covenant, namely Christmas and Easter While the New Testament shares the stories that are the focus of these two observances, it does not offer clear evidence that either were celebrated or were even known in the first century. The observance of Easter, referred to as "Pascha" by the early church, is only documented in the second century (in Asia Minor) and the first sure evidence of Christians celebrating the Lord's Nativity on December 25 comes in the fourth century.[39] Although grounded in the Christian Scriptures, the liturgical celebrations of both Christmas and Easter thus emerged after the appearance of New Testament literature.

What might we conclude about sacred time in the New Testament? For sure, there is not enough evidence to suggest that the earliest Christians followed any kind of highly developed liturgical calendar with an annual cycle of feasts—although they were clearly familiar with the Jewish calendar. But it does seem likely that at least some churches observed Sunday as a weekly day of worship in the mid- to late first century. While it would probably be reading too much into the New Testament to talk about a Christian

---

39. See Truscott, *Worship*, 113, 116.

liturgical calendar in the apostolic era, we can say that sacred time was part of the first-century Christian spiritual consciousness.

But what about certain negative statements in Pauline literature, viz., Galatians 4:10–11 ("You are observing special days and months and seasons and years! I fear that I have somehow wasted my efforts on you") and Colossians 2:16 ("Therefore let no one judge you by what you eat or drink, or with regard to a feast, a New Moon, or a Sabbath")? Regarding the former text, we must keep in mind the larger issue in Galatia, namely, that Christians there had adopted a legalistic brand of Christianity although they had been set free from the law by Jesus, who had made them true children of God (3:24; 4:5). Thus, Paul's purpose here is really to condemn the abandonment of the gospel itself rather than the observance of sacred time, which in this case is really only a symptom of a larger problem.

Similarly, regarding the Colossians text, the point is not to denigrate sacred time, but to say that a Christian's inclusion among the people of God cannot be based on adherence to Jewish time customs, which are only shadows of future realities (v. 17). According to N. T. Wright, although it might seem that Paul is contrasting "outward material regulations" with "inward spiritual truths," Paul is not really saying that Christians should have nothing to do with outward forms of worship. Wright argues that Colossians 2:17 is not a condemnation of things material and outward since (1) Christianity also affirms the material world, (2) verse 18 is actually a condemnation of nonmaterial aspects of the teaching opposed by Paul, (3) Paul's real point is to contrast the previous age (with its "shadows") with the coming age (of Christ), and (4) the "shadow/reality" language is used by Paul to argue that Christians need not cling to Jewish practices in order to be complete as people of God.[40] For these reasons we should not strain the meaning of the Colossians passage by making it into a polemic against the observance of sacred time.

With regard to sacred time, what we have in the New Testament, I would argue, is really the foundation for later developments. Jewish sacred time lays the groundwork for Christianity to eventually adopt its own calendar with the remembrance of Christ's birth and resurrection as its two anchoring points. Like the Jewish people, Christians would come to observe certain days in order to share the stories of their salvation history, both for their own spiritual edification and for their witness in the world. The rituals of these days, most especially baptism and the Lord's

40. Wright, *Colossians and Philemon*, 119–20.

Supper, would serve to imprint the Jesus story on the hearts and minds of converts by offering them bodily participation in the mystery of Jesus through washing and eating. The teaching of Paul, however, will serve as a corrective to any thought that the ritual observance of sacred time somehow justifies the Christian before God—as if the saving work of Jesus by itself were insufficient for salvation.

Sacred Space in the New Testament

The New Testament does not offer any comprehensive teaching on the matter of sacred space, nor does there seem to be any particular interest in the subject. The presence of the temple and synagogue were taken for granted, and both were utilized by the earliest Christians as places of worship and instruction. We have already mentioned how the temple and synagogue figured in the ministry of Jesus and his disciples. What is striking in the New Testament is the "spiritualizing" of the temple, which seems to revolve around two main ideas.

First, there is an identification of Jesus himself with the temple. Jesus' saying, "Destroy this temple, and I will raise it again in three days" (John 2:19), is understood as a reference to Jesus' own body and his death and resurrection (vv. 21–22). Thus, Jesus himself is a replacement for the temple because it is through him that God is encountered and human sin atoned for. Indeed, regarding atonement, John's Gospel refers to Jesus as the lamb of God who takes away the sin of the world (1:29). This Jesus-as-new-temple theology has profound implications for the Christian view of ritual. If authentic ritual that negotiates the human-divine relationship was tied to a particular place in Jewish thinking, for Christians it is tied to a particular person (see John 4:21–24). Indeed, the premier rituals of the New Testament, baptism and the Lord's Supper, are bound up with the personal presence of Jesus who infuses these rituals with the saving power of his atoning death (Rom 6:1–4; 1 Cor 11:23–26).

A second reinterpretation of the temple is the idea that the Christian people themselves constitute a holy temple:

> Do you not know that you yourselves are God's temple, and that
> God's Spirit dwells in you? If anyone destroys God's temple, God
> will destroy him; for God's temple is holy, and you are that temple.
> (1 Cor 3:16–17; cf 6:19)

> As you come to Him, the living stone, rejected by men but chosen
> and precious in God's sight, you also, like living stones, are being
> built into a spiritual house to be a holy priesthood, offering spiri-
> tual sacrifices acceptable to God through Jesus Christ. (1 Pet 2:4–5)

The ritual implications of this idea are likewise profound: any place of worship for Christians is holy because of the people who occupy it, not because of its particular location. This means that (1) the purpose of a Christian worship space is primarily to accommodate the needs of the worshippers, and (2) rituals must be communal and participatory, as opposed to leader-centered.

This "spiritualization" of the temple by Christians, however, does not mean that designing and constructing places for worship is somehow un-Christian. While some acts of worship in the New Testament may have taken place outdoors (e.g., the preaching of Jesus, various baptisms), many took place in designated spaces, e.g., Jesus' meal with his disciples in the upper room (Matt 26:17–19), and the preaching of Paul that was accompanied by the "breaking of bread" (Acts 20). These narratives effectively sanctify space and authorize its use for Christians in their worship.

The doctrine of the incarnation—God's self-manifestation in the person of Jesus of Nazareth—also supports an intentional use of space for worship. The humanity of the second person of the Trinity (Jesus) not only affirms the goodness of the human body but also the reality that it occupies time and space, must be sheltered from the elements, and that spaces need to be organized so that the body's needs are met. In that case, Christians are not "unspiritual" if they perceive a need to design and build spaces for their ritual activities. Doing so is not only a universal human need—as the caves in Chauvet, France would indicate—but also an indication that we take our humanity seriously, as does God.

Life Cycle Rituals in the New Testament

Ordination

As we saw earlier, priests in the Old Testament were consecrated for their ministry in a series of elaborate rites. It cannot be surprising, then, that the early church designated people for ministry through ritual acts. According to Acts 6:6, the deacons selected to help in the distribution of food were set aside for their ministry through a laying on of hands administered by the apostles. Paul and Barnabas were likewise designated for their missionary work by this same gesture (Acts 13:3). Paul speaks of an imposition of hands on Timothy (1 Tim 4:14; 2 Tim 1:6), which the apostle associates with the impartation of the gifts for ministry, especially preaching and teaching. As a ritual gesture, the laying on of hands signifies not only the rite setting apart of a person for a particular ministerial office, but also the power and authority given by the Holy Spirit for that office. In the case of the deacons, the laying on of hands signified the presence of the Holy Spirit in the candidates, while for Saul and Barnabas, the gesture signified the Spirit's call to ministry (Acts 13:2). It is not entirely clear whether the New Testament teaches that the laying on of hands actually *confers* the Holy Spirit in the case of presbyteral (priestly) ordination, but the gesture clearly has that meaning in other instances (Acts 8:17; 9:17; 19:6). Besides hand-laying, prayer was also part of "ordination" in early Christian communities, as we can see in Acts 6:6 and Acts 13:3, but there are no indications as to the content of these prayers. We might note that Jesus prayed by himself on a mountain prior to selecting the twelve apostles (Luke 6:12), which suggests that the early church sought to imitate his action when it designated people for ministry.

The New Testament does not outline the entire shape of a person's journey to official ministry, but it does suggest a transformative journey nevertheless. The laying on of hands seems to mark a transitional point in a person's life, insofar as he thereafter takes on a new ministry with new responsibilities (Acts 6, 13). The fact that this early ordination is conferred by others in positions of ministry leadership (1 Tim 4:14) suggests that hand-laying is a gesture of welcome into a new order, or in Van Gennep's terms, a rite of "incorporation." Thus, ordination is the ritualization of a person's new identity as a minister, and hence is truly a "rite of passage."

Confession of Sins

According to the Gospels of Matthew and Mark, members of John the Baptizer's audience confessed their sins in preparation for the coming of the messiah (Matt 3:6; Mark 1:5). Hence, John's baptism is a "baptism of repentance for the forgiveness of sins" (Mark 1:4; Luke 3:3). In doing this, John's hearers acknowledged their need for a savior to deliver them from sin. Matthew's gospel does not specifically refer to John's baptism in this manner, but confession was nevertheless bound up with John's baptism. It is interesting to note that Luke does not explicitly indicate, as do Matthew and Mark, that the candidates for John's baptism actually confessed their sins; for that matter, none of the gospels tell us what these persons actually said by way of a confession of sins prior to receiving John's baptism. Perhaps the confession took the form of a prayer, drawing on the words of certain Old Testament psalms (e.g., Ps 32:5–6; 51:3–4).

Confession of sin was part of church life in the first century. In the account of Paul's work in Ephesus (Acts 19:18), persons who previously engaged in un-Christian activities confessed their sins (e.g., sorcery). The author of James exhorts his audience to engage in mutual confession that they might find healing (5:16). Implicit in Jesus' advice to seek reconciliation with others before making an offering is the need to confess one's sins against a neighbor (Matt 5:23–24). While the New Testament does not indicate that confessing sins before a church leader is essential, it nevertheless (1) offers the example of Simon the Sorcerer confessing before Peter (Acts 8:24), and (2) narrates Jesus' act of authorizing the disciples to forgive and retain sins (John 20:23). What form confession took in the early church is difficult to discern because of the lack of ritual details. But it was certainly the early church's way of enabling people to tell the truth about themselves so that they might appropriate the forgiveness of God mediated through the death and resurrection of Jesus. Confession was, to use Asad and Mitchell's term, a "technology" for achieving the honesty that was central to Christian identity.

Furthermore, it seems that the confession of sins had three specific functions in the New Testament era. First, because the stories of John the Baptizer connect it to baptism, confession served as a ritual of initiation. To be a member of the community looking for the eschatological savior, one had to confess the truth about one's sins and spiritual need for salvation. Second, confession was as a ritual of reconciliation. Jesus' instructions about confronting sinners in the community (Matt 18:15–20) imply that confessing one's sin to the church is sometimes necessary for maintaining right relationships in that community. In other words, the confession of sins was a spiritual practice used for maintaining peace and harmony in the church community. Third, confession was a ritual for healing (Jas 5:16) and spiritual renewal (1 John 1:8–10). To confess one's sins (and to receive forgiveness) is to find freedom from the powers of sin and guilt. Thus, confession functioned as a return to baptism where one became a new person (Titus 3:5) and was joined to a new community whose life and faith was grounded in Jesus Christ.

Today, the public worship services of almost all churches include a rite of corporate confession of sins. Protestants have generally eschewed private confession because of potential abuses. But a few Protestant churches today do provide rites of confession and forgiveness in their official worship books.[41] In the case of Lutherans, private confession before an ordained minister maintains a quasi-sacramental status because forgiving sins is understood to be rooted in the command and promise of Jesus (John 20:23) and because the word of absolution ultimately comes from God himself and thus serves as a means of grace for the penitent (person making confession). Most Protestants regard a corporate rite of confession as a necessary preparation for the celebration of Holy Communion, not so much as a "cleansing" to make participants worthy of communion but as a way of expressing the deep spiritual needs that are met in the Supper.

Healing

That Jesus of Nazareth enjoyed an enormous reputation as a healer is evidenced by the large crowds that brought their sick, crippled, and demonically possessed persons to him so that he could heal them and exorcize their demons (Matt 8:16–17; Mark 1:32–34; Luke 4:40–41). While Jesus' healing ministry was motivated by his personal compassion for those oppressed by illness or evil spirits (Matt 14:14, 20:34), it also had messianic overtones. In other words, Jesus' acts of healing witnessed to the presence of God's kingdom (Luke 11:20) and his identity as God's messiah sent to deliver people from various forms of oppression. Jesus' mandate concerning the mission of his disciples to Israel also included healing (Matt 10:5–15; Mark 6:7–13; Luke 9:1–6). The one and only healing gesture associated with Jesus himself is hand-laying (Luke 4:40)[42] while both hand-laying (Mark 16:18; Acts 28:8) and anointing (Mark 6:13) were administered by his disciples. The reasons for these particular gestures are obvious: touch is a natural way of expressing care and concern for another person, and oil has practical value in soothing wounds (Luke 10:34), and thus it has symbolic significance as

41. *Book of Common Prayer* (1979), 447–52; *Book of Common Worship*, 1023–24; *ELW*, 243–44.

42. Hand-laying is a common ritual gesture throughout the Bible, and is connected not only with healing, but also with acts of blessing (Gen 48:14), conferral of the Holy Spirit (Acts 8:19; 13:1), and designating (setting apart) persons for ministry in the church (1 Tim 4:14).

a natural element like water or bread. We might note that some gospel accounts do not mention *any* ritual gesture being used for healing, either by Jesus (Matt 4:23) or his disciples (Matt 10; Luke 9:6).

In James 5, we find a description of how healing is to be carried out in the church:

> Is any one of you sick? He should call the elders of the church to pray over him and anoint him with oil in the name of the Lord. And the prayer offered in faith will restore the one who is sick. The Lord will raise him up. If he has sinned, he will be forgiven.
>
> Therefore, confess your sins to each other and pray for each other so that you may be healed. The prayer of a righteous man has great power to prevail. (vv. 14–16)

Several things are notable about this passage. First, the ministry of healing is to include both prayer and, in line with Mark 6:13, anointing with oil. Second, it appears that the prayer, rather than the anointing, is the effective agent of healing, since the prayer will restore the person to health. Third, sin is brought into the picture not necessarily because sickness is viewed as the result of sin, but arguably because illness, sickness, and death, along with sin, are all signs of humanity frailty. We might note that death—the loss of immortality—was the penalty paid by the first couple for their disobedience (Gen 3:22–24), which naturally leads us to associate sin and the body's finitude.

That healing functions as a rite of passage is evident in the New Testament. In James 5 the key words are "restore the one who is sick." Ritualized healing, in other words, seeks to return a person to a state of health, just as the confession of sin seeks to restore community and relationships. That a person obtains a different place in society as a result of healing is indicated by those gospel accounts where a person either serves Jesus after being healed, as in the case of Peter's mother-in-law (Matt 8:15), or becomes a follower of Jesus after having been severely limited by illness or handicap, as in the case of the blind man, Bartimaeus (Mark 10:52). Indeed, these accounts may even suggest that ritualized healing not only enacts personal restoration, but perhaps also initiates a person into fellowship with Jesus and his community.

In the centuries following the New Testament, anointing of the sick evolved into what came to be known as "extreme unction"—essentially, the anointing of persons close to death. But this practice was assailed by the Protestant Reformers because, in their view, it lacked a clear scriptural basis and was contrary to reason, since most recipients were not in fact "raised up," but rather died eventually. Given Protestant skepticism about anointing, it is rather noteworthy that the 1549 *Book of Common Prayer* (Anglican) included an anointing in its service for the visitation of the sick,[43] although the gesture disappeared from subsequent versions of the prayer book. Due to the influence of the Pentecostal-charismatic movement, with its emphasis on healing, as well as a concern for holistic ministry, ritual healing experienced a revival in mainline Protestantism during the twentieth century. Today, the liturgical books of several Protestant denominations include public services of healing with both hand-laying and anointing as the principal ritual gestures.[44]

Marriage

The New Testament contains no material related to marriage rituals, but only teaching on the meaning of marriage. The main theological affirmations are that: (1) the marriage of a man and a woman was instituted at the creation (Matt 19:4–6a); (2) marriage involves an unbreakable bond (Matt 19:6b); and (3) the love and submission that is found in marriage is an image of Christ's love for the church and the church's submission to Christ (Eph 5:21–25).

While the New Testament does not make any ritual prescriptions for marriage, scattered texts offer glimpses of common nuptial practices—"rituals" in a loose sense. All of these were well known even before the advent of Christianity, including: (1) the bride bathing prior to the wedding (Eph 5:26–27); (2) the bride wearing fine clothes (Rev 19:8); (3) the groom and party processing to the home of the bride (Matt 9:15; 25:1–13); (4) the groom party bearing torches (Matt 25:7); and (5) the wedding feast (Matt 22:1–10).[45]

Although Matthew 19:6 ("what God has joined together, let no one separate") is a formula pronounced at many marriage ceremonies today, we should not assume that it was used ritually among first-century Christians. At that time, marriage was still only a series of domestic "rituals," and it was not until Martin Luther's marriage service of 1529 that this

43. *Book of Common Prayer* (1549), 78.

44. *Book of Common Prayer* (1979), 455–56; *Book of Common Worship*, 994; *United Methodist Book of Worship*, 620–21; *ELW*, 277.

45. Gehman, "Marriage," 590–92; Wright and Thompson, "Marriage," 732–36.

Scripture verse was used as a ritual formula.[46] Furthermore, we find no New Testament precursors to contemporary marriage rituals such as the consent to the marriage, vows, rings, or unity candles. Yet the journey of the groom to the home of the bride, and then back to his own home for the feast—ritualized movement—does suggest symbolically the passage from single to married status. Additionally, the feast serves as a welcome and incorporation of the couple into society as people with a new social status. The marriage feast will ultimately serve as an image of the redemption and new life won for humanity by Jesus, the Lamb of God (Rev 19:7, 9).

Death

Just as it contains no liturgy or rituals for marriage, so the New Testament offers no funeral service or even any hints about what should be the core rituals of a Christian funeral. As with marriage, we catch only a few glimpses of common mourning and burial customs, namely: (1) loud mourning taking place in the home of the deceased (Luke 8:52); (2) carrying the deceased on a bier (Luke 7:12); (3) wrapping the body in a linen cloth (Matt 27:59); (4) applying spices to the body (Luke 24:1); and (5) laying the body in the chamber of a hewn-out rock face (Matt 27:60). Although we might not consider these actions/gestures "rituals," we can sense the ritualization of a life passage nevertheless. The carrying of the deceased on a bier is not merely the removal of a dead body (for health reasons), but in actuality, it suggests the movement from life to death. In ritualizing this movement, the procession and other burial customs help mourners to accept their loved one's new status—although for Christians the passage ultimately leads to eternal life and membership with the saints who dwell with the Lord Jesus.

Rather than the rituals of death, the New Testament is more interested in the meaning of death in light of Jesus' resurrection, and the following affirmations are central to its teaching about death: (1) Jesus was raised from the dead having defeated the power of death (Rom 6:9); (2) the dead will be raised (1 Cor 15:12–32); (3) the dead will be united with Christ and with other faithful disciples at Jesus' second coming (1 Thess 4:13–18); and (4) all the dead will face a final judgement (John 5:28–29; Heb 6:2), with the righteous to receive eternal life and evildoers to be consigned to eternal death/separation from God (Matt 25:46). Many of the texts that serve as the basis for the Christian perspective on death have

46. Luther, *Order for Marriage for Common Pastors* (1529), *LW* 53:111–13.

been incorporated into funeral services either as liturgical formulae or Scripture readings, e.g., John 11:25 and 1 Corinthians 15:12–32. It is these texts as much as any ritual that offer Christians hope as they commend their dead to God and look for assurance in the face of death.

Conclusion: Is the New Testament Opposed to Ritual?

To some Christians, it might appear that the New Testament is inherently opposed to ritual—or is ambivalent on the matter. First, it offers few details about the central actions of Christian worship (baptism, the Lord's Supper), and, except for healing, gives no prescriptions about occasional rites (e.g., marriage, funerals). Second, Jesus himself criticized some of the ritualistic practices of the Pharisees in Matthew 23:23–26. However, if we look closely at this text, we see that what is condemned is not ritual per se, but the "neglect" of "justice, mercy, and faithfulness." Indeed, Jesus' words suggest that as long as the "weightier matters" of the law are practiced, tithing rituals are acceptable.

Also opposed to an anti-ritual reading of the New Testament is the fact that Jesus himself engaged in ritual. First, he probably administered baptisms (John 3, 4), and he clearly authorized his disciples to baptize (Matt 28). Second, he celebrated the Passover with his disciples and commanded them to continue holding a ritual meal in memory of him. Third, Jesus observed the sacred times of the Jewish liturgical calendar, as evidenced by his three appearances in Jerusalem at Passover (John 2:23; 6:4; 13:1). Fourth, in giving thanks over the bread and cup during the meal in the upper room with his disciples, Jesus likely used traditional prayer forms, viz., a prayer of thanksgiving that praised God for creation and salvation and petitioned the fulfillment of God's promises for the future. Fifth, Jesus instructed his disciples concerning certain ritual matters, namely, prayer, fasting, and the giving of alms (Matt 6). Sixth, his use of hand-laying in connection with healing indicates an acceptance of traditional ritual gestures. The fact that the disciples' healing ministry involved anointing only confirms that Jesus and his inner circle of followers were users of ritual.

Even so, could we not historically relativize the rituals of the New Testament by suggesting that passages dealing with baptism and the Lord's Supper (especially) are merely descriptions of practices that were not meant to be normative for Christians of all times and places? Such an understanding is hardly plausible, because ritual is bound up with sacred story. If Christians were to share the good news of Jesus to the ends of the earth (Acts 1:8), they would necessarily have to share the ritual means by which people come to indwell that story, namely, baptism and the Supper. The imperative to make disciples of all nations (Matt 28:19–20) included the handing over of the ritual that initiated people into the Jesus story, namely, baptism.

Moreover, people in the ritually attuned world of the ancient Near East would have been looking for rituals to allow them personal and bodily participation in the Christian gospel story. Most likely, they would have rejected a religious movement that was a- or anti-ritualistic—a reality not lost on the authors and compilers of the New Testament. Indeed, it would not be far-fetched to suggest that Christianity's missionary "success" in the ancient world was due to its ritual repertoire, one that was grounded in and relevant to everyday life, but not so elaborate as to overwhelm new converts. If we recognize that ritual is a human universal, since we can only relate to transcendent realities through rituals that act on our bodies, it is nearly impossible to think that the rituals of the New Testament can be jettisoned in favor of a supposedly purer, unritualized form of Christianity.

I conclude this chapter with a summary of the information on ritual we find in the New Testament:

1. The New Testament identifies the core rituals of Christian worship. Although we cannot be sure about all the ritual details, the multiple references to baptism and the Lord's Supper suggest that early Christian worship revolved around these actions and that these shaped the faith and life of the church. There can be no doubt that baptism and the Lord's Supper were to be perpetuated in the life of church, insofar as they were authorized by the Lord Jesus and are connected with his very presence in the church.

2. The New Testament offers glimpses of other rituals and ritual gestures used by early Christians. It is clear that the ministry of healing involved hand-laying and anointing with oil, along with prayer. We can also say for certain that formal acts of "ordination" were known in the middle of the first century, and involved the laying on of hands and prayer. Less certain is whether the confession of sins involved ritual gestures.

3. The New Testament reinterprets sacred space, but does not reject it. While there is no theology of sacred space in the New Testament, there is a theology of holy people who occupy space. Jesus himself is

a replacement for the temple—a new means of encountering God—because his once-for-all sacrifice makes the temple obsolete. He and his people together constitute a new temple. Yet the earliest followers of Jesus did not eschew traditional sacred spaces (temple and synagogue), but made use of them for worship and evangelization. The doctrine of the incarnation not only affirms and sanctifies the human body, but also the spaces used by it and the need for the intentional organization of physical space for the worship of God.

4. The New Testament implicitly affirms the reckoning of sacred time. While nothing suggests that the earliest Christians observed their own liturgical calendar, they were clearly aware of the Jewish calendar, and did not condemn it. Statements by Paul that seem negative about observing sacred time need to be read within the context of his overall point about avoiding legalism.

When it came to the reformation of the church in the sixteenth century, the Reformers turned to the Bible for guidance, believing it to be the sole norm for church practice. Such was especially true of Martin Luther and John Calvin, whose teachings on ritual will be the subject of the next chapter.

Chapter 5

Martin Luther and John Calvin on Ritual in Christian Worship

Introduction

IN THE PREVIOUS CHAPTER we considered the role of ritual for the ancient Jewish people and then the place of ritual in the early church. Especially in the case of the former, we saw a spiritual/cultural life that revolved around rituals. While early Christians rejected some Jewish rituals because of the belief that a new era had dawned and had necessarily abrogated certain aspects of the old covenant, early Christian worship also revolved around rituals, in particular an initiatory bath (baptism) and a regular fellowship meal that pointed to Jesus' death and his promise to return in glory. Ritual components that are universals in faith communities continued to be used by early Christians even with their sense of eschatological newness and discontinuity.

While it would be a noble goal to chronicle the evolution of the church's teaching about ritual, such an effort is not within the scope of the present volume. Instead, we will explore the thinking of two important figures who arose at a decisive point in the history of the church, namely, the Protestant Reformers Martin Luther and John Calvin, considered the "founders" of their respective branches of Protestantism. What they offer us is a way of thinking about ritual that mirrors that of the earliest Christians: continuity in discontinuity. Both Reformers shared an interest in the Bible, biblical preaching, and theology that effectively deconstructed the old ritual life that many Christians found oppressive. Yet both could speak positively about ritual and sought to clarify its role in the life of the church. Additionally, their criticisms of the sixteenth-century church give us a glimpse of this church's ritual life, albeit a prejudiced one. So, we will explore their views in the hope that they might instruct us and help us form our own perspectives on ritual in Christian public worship.

Martin Luther on Ritual in Christian Worship

The name Martin Luther (1483–1546) is synonymous with the Protestant Reformation in Germany during the first half of the sixteenth century. His writings, teaching, and translation of the Bible were the basis for a confessional movement that was both evangelical and catholic. Much of his critique of the late medieval church focused on the sacraments and ritual aspects of church life. His treatise *The Babylonian Captivity of the Church* (1520) is considered Protestantism's definitive deconstruction of the medieval church's sacramental system. Yet the blistering criticisms contained in this work should not blind us to the fact that Luther made positive contributions to the ritual/sacramental life of those churches influenced by him. His *Order of Mass and Communion for the Church at Wittenberg* or *Formulae missae* (1523) and *German Mass* or *Deutsche Messe* (1526) served as guides for the celebration of an evangelical mass that highlights the saving gifts of Jesus Christ. The German baptismal rites (1523, 1526) prepared by Luther cleared away much of the ritual clutter of the ages and placed the bath itself (by immersion) at the heart of the service. The occasional services developed by Luther (ordination, marriage, private confession, and absolution) bear the stamp of a theology that is thoroughly biblical and pastoral. His hymns infused services not only with well-crafted music, but also with words expressive of the Reformation's core teachings. Thus, Luther himself played a central role in shaping the ritual life of Protestant Christians both during his time and beyond.

This is hardly surprising given Luther's own ritual formation prior to the Reformation. His deep interest in matters liturgical and sacramental owes in large part to his own spiritual formation as a Catholic Christian and a member of a monastic order. During his years as an Augustinian hermit (1505 to 1525), Luther experienced a life punctuated by the services of the Divine Office (aka "Daily Prayer"), whereby he and fellow friars offered prayer and praise in the midst of daily life. Prompted by a conscience troubled by sin, he frequently sought private confession before his monastic superior, Johann von Staupitz. As a priest and parish pastor he presided at the mass, preached, and conducted the various occasional rites. He also had familiarity with all the ritual aspects of church life outside of the mass: benediction of the blessed sacrament (i.e., blessing a worship assembly with a consecrated host), processions on feast days (e.g., Corpus Christi), Marian rituals, pilgrimages to holy sites (especially those associated with saints), and the cult of relics that flourished in Germany during his time.

Luther's own devotion to the saints is evidenced by his invocation of St. Anna to preserve him from a thunderstorm in 1510—the very occasion that prompted him to cease law studies and enter an Augustinian monastery. Five years later, a business trip to Rome enabled him to experience the liturgical and devotional life of Western Christendom's holiest city, especially its papal rituals. As a student and teacher, he knew well the sacramental theology of the Middle Ages, especially that of Peter Lombard (1096–1160), whose *Sentences* was a standard textbook. Thus, when Luther wrote on ritual and sacramental matters he did so as one with knowledge and experience in this area. Especially because of the profound theological perspective that he gained from biblical studies, his teaching about ritual reflects well-formed convictions, not merely his personal preferences. Accordingly, what Luther teaches about ritual has to be taken seriously by Christians today. Thankfully, we find in him someone with a balanced view on ritual. While he assailed ritual practices that he viewed as abusive or erroneous, he nevertheless valued ritual, and so was both prophet and apologist in this area. Accordingly, we will examine his richly nuanced position on ritual in the hope of gaining our own balanced view.

To begin with, we must recognize the important distinction that he makes between ceremonies and signs. "Ceremony" is actually used in a dual sense by Luther. First, he employs the term to refer to priestly gestures in the mass and to actions like the laying on of hands in confirmation or the blessing of water.[1] Second, he uses "ceremony" in reference to external structures and liturgical paraphernalia that are "outwardly necessary or useful, proper and good—for instance, certain holidays, certain hours . . . set aside for preaching and praying, or the use of a church building or house, altar, pulpit, baptismal font, candlesticks, candles, bells, priestly vestments and the like."[2]

Such things are not necessary for salvation in the sense that they justify us before God, but they are "necessary" for the existence and survival of the church and for "good order" (1 Cor 14:40).[3] Luther likens the ritual/

---

1. Luther, *Babylonian Captivity* (1520), *AL* 3:54, 96.

2. Luther, *Councils and the Church* (1539), *AL* 3:438.

3. Luther, *Councils and the Church*, *AL* 3:438.

ceremonial aspects of Christian public worship to the models or plans used by builders and artisans. While such plans are not permanent and are not the real thing, they are still necessary because nothing can be built without them. Although they are set aside after the structure is completed, they are not despised but are sought after again and again. Similarly, outward ceremonies are not the true substance of Christian life and worship, but they are valued because they point to Christian truths. Accordingly, we should not reject ceremonies, but rather we should reject the erroneous idea that they are the basis of true righteousness.[4] Because ceremonies are of human origin,[5] they should not be rigidly imposed on Christians by authorities (e.g., bishops), such that they become burdensome. Churches should have the flexibility to change ceremonies from time to time.[6]

In contrast to ceremonies are the "signs" that bear God's salvific promises to humanity. These signs are actions that involve tangible things. For example, the "sign" of Holy Communion is the eating and drinking of the bread and wine that are the bearers of Christ's body and blood, while the "sign" of baptism is the immersion in water that joins one to Christ's death and resurrection.[7] For Luther, sacramental signs were also part of the old covenant. Any time God makes a promise, the Reformer says, God also gives a sign that serves as a memorial or remembrance of that promise. For example, after God promised Noah that he would never again destroy the earth, God gave the sign of the rainbow (Gen 9:12–13). After promising to make Abraham the "father of many nations," God then gave Abraham circumcision as a sign of the covenant between them (Gen 17:11).[8]

The signs with their corresponding promises, whether of the old covenant or the new covenant, are saving, because they evoke the faith that puts a person into a right relationship with God (cf. Gen 15:6). Thus, the efficacy of Christian sacraments consists not in the sign (action) itself, but in the faith that the participant has in the promise that is attached to that sign. "Not the sacrament, but the faith of the sacrament justifies."[9] By

4. Luther, *Freedom of a Christian* (1520), *AL* 1:536–37

5. Luther states that the holiness of the church does not consist in the rituals and ceremonies ("surplices, tonsures, long albs, or other ceremonies") that the papacy has "invented over and above the Holy Scriptures." *Smalcald Articles* (1537), *BC*, 325.3.

6. Luther, *Councils and the Church*, *AL* 3:411.

7. Luther, *Babylonian Captivity*, *AL* 3:46.

8. Luther, *Babylonian Captivity*, *AL* 3:46.

9. Quoted by Luther in *Babylonian Captivity*, *AL* 3:68.

contrast, mere ceremonies (or "legal symbols") have no word of promise from God, do not evoke a faith that justifies, and are fulfilled in their mere observance apart from any faith.[10]

For Luther, the sacraments (baptism and the Lord's Supper) do more than merely distinguish Christians from non-Christians, "for those who believe the promise and make use of these signs become the people of God and are saved."[11] Ultimately, sacramental signs (water, bread, wine) signify God's own help to save humanity from his wrath and condemnation, in contrast to all of humanity's self-chosen ways of salvation that are nothing more than forms of false worship. Accordingly, the Reformer says: "[God] wants us to be gathered in connection with the word and baptism as by a sure and infallible sign because he wants to save and help us, just as he promises he would listen at the mercy seat among the people of Israel."[12]

But why have *any* external ritualistic activity in worship, whether ceremonies or sacramental signs, if believing God's promises is the one and only thing that justifies? For one thing, it is a matter of how God desires to encounter humanity. According to Luther, out of consideration for human weakness and inability to experience God in his true majesty,

> God wants to work through tolerable, kind, and pleasant means, which we ourselves could not have chosen better. He has, for instance, a godly and kind man speak to us, preach, lay his hands on us, remit sin, baptize, give us bread and wine to eat and drink. Who can be terrified by these pleasing methods, and wouldn't rather delight in them with all his heart?[13]

In other words, ritual signs and ceremonies are an accommodation to human nature, otherwise we would be frightened and overwhelmed by the presence of God if God were to deal with us directly. Perhaps one of Luther's better-known statements on God's ritual accommodation of humanity is in the *Large Catechism*, where he offers an apologetic for the external nature of baptism against Reformers who taught that faith needs no externals signs or ceremonies:

> Our know-it-alls . . . claim that faith alone saves and that works and external things add nothing to it. We answer: It is true, nothing

---

10. Luther, *Babylonian Captivity*, AL 3:69.
11. Luther, *Lectures on Genesis Chapters 15–20*, LW 3:110.
12. Luther, *Lectures on Genesis Chapters 26–30*, LW 5:128.
13. Luther, *Councils and the Church*, AL 3:436.

that is in us does it but faith. . . . But these leaders of the blind are unwilling to see that faith must have something to believe—something to which it may cling and upon which it may stand. Thus, faith clings to the water and believes it to be baptism, in which there is sheer salvation and life, not through the water, as we have sufficiently stated, but through its incorporation with God's Word and ordinance and the joining of his name to it.

. . . Yes, it must be external so that it can be perceived and grasped by the senses and thus brought into the heart, just as the entire gospel is an external, oral proclamation. In short, whatever God does and effects in us he desires to accomplish through such an external ordinance.[14]

Signs and ceremonies are of such importance that Luther can state that God "reveals himself through the word, signs, wonders, rites, ceremonies, that [humans] may know that he is present everywhere, *and may all but feel him with their hands.*"[15]

Ceremonies also serve a pedagogical purpose in church life. This aspect of ritual, already at work in the Old Testament,[16] is particularly crucial for the youth of the church. According to Luther, young people need to be trained by the "iron bars" of ceremonies, "so that their unrestrained heart may not go blindly into corruption."[17] Yet youth should never be misled into thinking that the observance of ceremonies justifies them before God.[18] Rather, they should be taught that the purpose of ceremonies is to help them avoid sin and learn to recognize what the true basis of justification is. In Luther's view, ritual formation principally involves children and takes place in schools and homes, as when children are taught to bend the knee at the name of Jesus.[19]

One of Luther's chief criticisms of the medieval church is its excessive number of (unnecessary) rituals. While he did not think that the church should be faulted for adding various ceremonies to the mass over the years, he also believed that these could obscure the true substance of

---

14. Luther, *Large Catechism* (1529), *BC* 460.28–30.

15. Luther, *Lectures on Genesis Chapters 6–14*, *LW* 2:255. Emphasis added.

16. Luther sees the building of temples and the "proliferation of ceremonies" in the Old Testament as a kind of "pedagogy" through which God "attracts and invites us to Himself." *Lectures on Genesis Chapters 21–25*, *LW* 4 322.

17. Luther, *Freedom of a Christian*, *AL* 1:536

18. Luther, *Freedom of a Christian*, *AL* 1:536

19. Luther, *Councils of the Church*, *AL* 3:411.

the mass, which was the distributing of Christ's testament (promise) to God's people.[20] But baptism also suffered from ritual overload in his view. Hence, after producing a German-language baptism service in 1523 that made few changes over the Latin rite, Luther later published a revised service (1526) that removed many of the traditional secondary ceremonies (e.g., the blowing in the face of the child, the giving of salt, the opening of the candidate's ears). In fact, he had already expressed doubts about the necessity of these "external" embellishments in the instructions that accompanied his 1523 baptismal service.[21] What remained in the revised order of 1526 were the marking with the sign of the cross (to begin the rite), a hand-laying during the recitation of the Lord's Prayer, the washing (by immersion), and the conferral of a baptismal garment.[22]

Another issue for Luther was that some rituals were taking on more importance than was justifiable. For example, he argues that the consecration of priests ("clerics") by anointing had been accorded greater significance than baptism, such that priests were given a higher status than all other baptized Christians. He states that there could really be no comparison in this case since baptism constitutes a washing in the blood of Christ and an anointing with the Holy Spirit, while clerical anointing was an act of human origin that lacked a divine command.[23] Furthermore, while clerical anointing was only for the purpose of saying masses, baptism was for eternal life. The supposed higher status of clergy was further underscored through (1) special garb and tonsures that gave the impression that priests "belonged" to Christ, and (2) the teaching that priests received a spiritual mark on the soul, which no ordinary Christian had. Since it really served the private mass business, priestly anointing was essentially bound up with theological error and ecclesiastical abuse, since private mass lacked a foundation in God's Word, offered sacrifices God, and made the mass into a good work. Thus, for Luther ritual had to serve true worship.

Another misuse of ritual according to Luther is "the various ways of trusting in works and ceremonies"—in other words, regarding mere ceremonies as necessary for salvation.[24] For this error Luther holds the papacy responsible:

---

20. Luther, *Babylonian Captivity*, AL 3:54.

21. Luther, *Order of Baptism* (1523), LW 53:102.

22. Luther, *Order of Baptism Newly Revised* (1526), LW 53:107–9.

23. Luther, *Private Mass and the Consecration of Priests* (1533), LW 38:185.

24. Luther, *Babylonian Captivity*, AL 3:90.

> We are indebted to you, O Roman See, and to your murderous
> laws and ceremonies, with which you corrupted all [humankind],
> so that they believe that they can with works make satisfaction
> for sin to God, when God can be satisfied only by the faith of a
> contrite heart.[25]

Any teaching that ceremonies are necessary for salvation had two significant implications. First, it robbed Christians of their freedom, which for Luther was at the heart of Christian identity.[26] This freedom, naturally, is lived out in the use of rituals, as he suggests in the following remarks on ceremonial matters in the *Formula missae*:

> Thus we think about [the celebration of] the mass. But in all
> these matters we will want to beware lest we make binding what
> should be free, or make sinners of those who may do some things
> differently or omit others. . . . For these rites are supposed to be
> for Christians, i.e., children of the "free woman" [Gal 4:31], who
> observe them voluntarily and from the heart, but are free to
> change them how and whenever they may wish. Therefore, it is
> not in these matters that anyone should either seek or establish
> as law some indispensable form by which he might ensnare or
> harass consciences.[27]

Second, requiring ceremonies as though they were necessary for salvation fostered false worship, a reality brought about by the devil:

> Wherever Christ builds a temple and gathers a church, Satan in-
> variably has the habit of imitating him like an ape and inventing
> idolatrous forms of worship and idolatrous traditions similar to
> the true doctrine and true forms of worship. But he belittles the
> promise and the spirit of the fathers, and meanwhile he introduced
> impressive pomp and magnificent pageantry. The result is that he

25. Luther, *Babylonian Captivity*, AL 3:93.

26. Along these lines Luther writes: "Our freedom has as its foundation Christ, who is the eternal High Priest, who is at the right hand of God and intercedes for us. Therefore, the freedom, forgiveness of sins, righteousness, and life that we have through him are sure, firm, and eternal, provided that we believe this. If we cling firmly to Christ by faith and stand firm in the freedom with which he has made us free, we shall have those inestimable gifts. But if we become smug and drowsy, we shall lose them. It is not in vain that Paul commands us to be vigilant and to stand, because he knows that the devil is busily engaged in trying to rob us of this freedom that cost Christ so much, and to tie us up again in the yoke of slavery through his agents." *Lectures on Galatians Chapters 5–6* (1535), *LW* 27:6.

27. Luther, *Order of Mass and Communion*, LW 53:30–31.

> overcomes and obscures true worship and the church by means of
> a semblance of religion and saintliness.[28]

Besides making distinctions between ceremonies and signs, and between true and false ritual/worship, Luther also makes distinctions between those who misuse ritual. First are people who, in an effort to establish their Christian freedom, despise all ceremonies and ecclesiastical traditions, as if the essence of being a Christian is *not* fasting, or *not* using prescribed prayers, etc. Second are persons who, by contrast, think that all rituals are absolutely necessary and contribute to one's eternal salvation. Both groups share the common error of neglecting "the more serious things that are necessary for salvation."[29] Paul, however, provides a middle way between both camps. According to Luther, Romans 14:3 ("Let him who eats . . ."), rules out any despising of ceremonies, while at the same time suggesting that hard-core ceremonialists refrain from judging others. Luther faults both parties for failing to exercise mutual love. Neither group can claim that their position justifies them before God.[30] Luther suggests that while bodily life requires the use of rituals that appeal to the senses, righteousness before God is not bound up with this dependence on ritual.

Luther offers advice on how to respond to both ritualists and anti-ritualists. First, he counsels that Christians intentionally "offend" ceremonialists by eating meat, breaking fasts, and doing other things that they would consider sinful.[31] Such persons need to be taught that their "laws" contribute nothing toward righteousness and should never have been set up in the first place.[32] Luther finds a precedent for this approach in Paul's refusal to circumcise Titus in the face of those who insisted that he do so (Gal 2:3). Second, Christians must avoid offending those who cannot appreciate the liberty of faith. To the contrary, we should "yield" to their weakness so that they might be amenable to further instruction. Luther argues that such persons are not "stubbornly wicked," but simply "weak in the faith" and in many cases are the victims of pastors who use ceremonial traditions to control them.

But finding a middle way was sometimes complicated for Luther, as in the case of the elevation—the traditional gesture whereby the

---

28. Luther, *Lectures on Genesis Chapters 21–25, LW* 4:236.

29. Luther, *Freedom of a Christian, AL* 1:531.

30. Luther, *Freedom of a Christian, AL* 1:532.

31. Luther, *Freedom of a Christian, AL* 1:533.

32. Luther, *Freedom of a Christian, AL* 1:535.

priest-celebrant raises the consecrated elements during the eucharistic prayer. In the *Formula missae* he states that the gesture should be retained for the sake of the weak in faith.[33] In a later work he states that although he was inclined to drop the gesture, he retained it because his former teaching colleague in Wittenberg, Andreas von Karlstadt (1486–1541), viewed it as a great sin. For his part, Luther regarded the elevation as a "matter of indifference"—something that was neither commanded nor forbidden, but left free.[34] Yet because his Roman Catholic opponents seemed to make this gesture necessary for salvation, Luther did not want to retain it out of compulsion. Ultimately, Luther discarded the elevation because many (Protestant) churches had done so and because he desired unity and harmony in the church. He states that:

> For where [the elevation] can be done without sin and endangering the conscience or without giving offense, it is indeed fine for the churches to agree in external matters, which are in many cases voluntary, even as they agree with one another in the Spirit, in the faith, in the word, and the sacrament; for such an agreement makes a fine impression and pleases everyone.[35]

By way of summary, we highlight three central themes in Luther's teaching on ritual:

1. Justification. What propelled Luther into his work as a Reformer was his "discovery" of the Pauline doctrine of justification, i.e., Paul's teaching that faith, rather than "works of the law," places a person in right relationship with God (Rom 3:21–24; 5:9–11). For Luther, everything in his teaching depended on this article.[36] So it is not surprising that the church's ritual—the means of enacting its faith—would be evaluated through the lens of justification. Essentially, he applies the doctrine of justification when he states that neither a dogged insistence on a ritual for its own sake nor a despising of ritual in general justifies a person before God. Only a faith that receives the promises that God makes through his appointed signs justifies a person.

---

33. Luther, *Order of Mass and Communion for the Church at Wittenberg* (1523), *LW* 53:28.

34. Luther, *Brief Confession* (1544), *LW* 38:316.

35. Luther, *Brief Confession, LW* 38:316–17.

36. Luther, *Smalcald Articles, BC,* 3C1.5.

2. Freedom. For Luther, Christ, gospel, freedom, and worship all go together. Yet the Christians of his day were being robbed of their freedom by an excessive number of ceremonies and by pressure to adhere to them. In reaction, Luther stressed freedom in ritual matters. But such freedom was tempered by love for the neighbor and harmony in the church—biblical teachings that were equally important to him. Significantly, Luther never sought the complete abolition of all rituals as staunch despisers of ritual might have desired. As a realist, Luther knew that "ceremonies" would have to be a part of church life as long as it exists in this world.

3. Love. The danger in making use of one's Christian freedom is that one might confuse and alienate persons who do not appreciate the Christian's freedom in ritual matters. Or worse, the "free" person might lead the "weak in faith" to do things that would trouble their consciences. Luther's insistence that reform not scandalize the "weak" draws on Paul's counsel to the Corinthians to avoid eating meat sacrificed to idols if doing so would harm the consciences of the weak (1 Cor 8). Such concern for the neighbor is born of love, which is the practical outgrowth of one's faith in God (1 John 2:9–11). We find the love ethic at work in a series of sermons that Luther preached in Wittenberg during Lent 1522, in which he counseled against violent reform and iconoclasm, all in effort to restore order following social disturbances. In the first of these he accuses his audience of failing to exhibit mutual love.[37] The following day, he addresses the matter of private masses, stating that while he agrees that these should be abolished, they should not be ended by force. Instead, God's Word should be preached and Christians should rely on this action alone to correct the problem.[38]

For Luther, refraining from the forceful suppression of traditional rituals is not only a loving service to the neighbor, but also to God, whose Word alone is the true source of ritual reform. While that Word might condemn erroneous ritual practices, it also expresses God's love for broken sinners and naturally inspires love for the neighbor, even the spiritually "weak" neighbor who has not fully appropriated the meaning of the gospel.

37. Luther, *Invocavit Sermons* (First Sermon, 9 March 1522), *AL* 4:15.
38. Luther, *Invocavit Sermons* (Second Sermon, 10 March 1522), *AL* 4:20.

John Calvin on Ritual

John Calvin (1509–1564) was born in Noyon, France, and spent his early life in Paris studying for the priesthood and then later received legal training. A conversion led him away from his original academic path to an intense study of the Bible. In 1536, he produced the first version of his *Institutes of the Christian Religion*, a systematic theology covering the doctrines of God, salvation, the church, and the Christian life. After a brief ministry in Geneva, he engaged in pastoral work in Strasburg (1538–1541), under the supervision of the German Reformer Martin Bucer (1491–1551), before returning to Geneva to undertake the reform of both church and society. Through preaching and teaching that sought to expound the will of God for humanity, he exerted a strong and lasting influence. He produced commentaries on almost every book of the Bible, and was interested in the exact meaning of texts, which led him to pay particular attention to the historical and theological backgrounds of texts. Yet Calvin always interpreted particular passages in light of the whole message of the Bible.[39]

As a theologian, Calvin, like Luther, was particularly interested in the doctrine of justification, and also like the Wittenberg Reformer, was a keen student of Augustine. While we associate Calvin with the doctrines of the sovereignty of God and predestination, many scholars would insist that neither of these themes dominated his thinking. We should note that his teaching on predestination was particularly controversial because his belief that God rejected those without faith (the non-elect) seemed to contradict the freedom of God and to undermine some of his teachings on God. But Calvin's theology was always a work in progress, as evidenced by the publication of a second edition of the *Institutes* in 1559. His theological orientation is clearly evident when it comes to ritual: he rejected all practices that he deemed unscriptural, and, in accordance with his doctrine of justification, he denied that any ritual could merit eternal salvation, since this matter rested entirely on God's grace. For Calvin, worship should be reformed according to the Scriptures, but also in continuity with the ancient church.

Calvin's thoughts about the ritualistic aspect of Christian life and public worship are found in numerous works, most notably in his *Institutes*. For him certain ritual actions are necessary for salvation (preaching of the Word, sacraments), and these have been explicitly commanded by

---

39. Wallace, "Calvin, John," 143–47.

God.[40] Calvin recognizes two other types of rituals, both of which have an important role in the church: those that provide for decorum (e.g., kneeling, praying with an uncovered head, administering the sacraments and burying the dead in a dignified manner, fasting, and excommunication), and those that provide for order (e.g., set hours for public prayer and preaching, the observance of silence at certain points in public worship services, and set days for the celebration of the Lord's Supper).[41] He understands, however, that some ritual actions cannot be categorized as *either* divinely commanded or humanly derived. Kneeling, he says, is both: it is divine, since it is a type of decorum recommended by the apostles, and yet it is human because it was something done out of a general understanding rather than in response to an explicit command of God.

Furthermore, he argues that God did not desire to prescribe every ceremonial aspect of church life since God knew that such matters would have to be determined by the local context. Thus, the church should make ceremonial decisions based on what it needs for decency and good order. Because ceremonial matters are not necessary for salvation and reflect local circumstances, the church may in some cases abolish old ceremonies and introduce new ones, although these actions are not undertaken capriciously.[42] Finally, Calvin holds that those rites and ceremonies needed for good order in the church are not efficacious in and of themselves. The power and efficacy of the apostolic laying on of hands for the consecration of deacons, he contends, is dependent on the work of the Holy Spirit. This is indicated by the fact that the consecration also required prayer (Acts 6:6).[43]

But if rituals are to be founded on God's Word, and if the Old Testament contains many rituals that were commanded by God, is not the church then obligated to follow all of the ceremonial/ritual practices of the old covenant? For Calvin the answer is "no." In the first place he holds that the rituals of the Old Testament were purely spiritual, that is to say, they pointed beyond themselves to realities yet to be fulfilled in Jesus Christ. As such, they were only temporary until his coming. Thus "their true perpetuity consists in their being abrogated by the coming of

40. "Because the Lord, in his holy oracles, has faithfully comprehended and plainly declared to us the whole nature of true righteousness, and all the parts of Divine worship, with whatever is necessary to salvation—in these he is to be regarded as our only Master." Calvin, *Institutes*, IV.x.30.

41. Calvin, *Institutes*, IV.x.29.

42. Calvin, *Institutes*, IV.x.30.

43. Calvin, *Commentary on the Acts of the Apostles 1–13*, 163.

Christ; because from then on it follows that their virtues and purpose are established in Christ."[44] Indeed, the worship of the Old Testament was only temporary and effectively ended with Christ.[45]

For Calvin, ritual is used rightly when participants are fully engaged. Singing, he says, is a completely useless endeavor unless the words and their vocalization through song truly come from the singer's heart (cf. Isa 29:13).[46] This means that the mind remains on God and one is not distracted. Similarly, in regard to liturgical prayer he states that "the tongue without the mind must be highly displeasing to God," and that "the mind ought to be kindled with an ardor of thought so as far to surpass all that the tongue can express by speaking."[47]

Furthermore, rituals must not be observed under compulsion; in other words, there should not be laws and regulations that compel Christians to worship in ways not commanded by God such that Christian liberty is destroyed.[48] Yet freedom does not mean that Christians can despise rituals or take a cavalier attitude toward them. While Christians recognize that some rituals are not fixed forever, they should also realize that rituals are needed because of human weakness, and so adhere to them out of mutual love for their fellow Christians. While a person does not sin when failing to observe a traditional custom like kneeling during prayer due to forgetfulness or infirmity, refusing to observe a custom out of contempt is never acceptable.[49]

We should also note that Calvin exhibited some flexibility when counseling Christians who lived in un-Reformed ecclesiastical contexts. In his view these Christians could observe those ceremonies not "stamped with impiety," so long as they could do so with freedom and without anxiety in order "to make manifest that [they] have no superstition either in observing or refraining from them."[50] However, they were to avoid all ceremonies that even hinted of something sacrilegious, including "worship

44. Calvin, *Commentary on the Acts of the Apostles 1–13*, 169–70.

45. Calvin, *Commentary on the Acts of the Apostles 14–28*, 64.

46. Calvin, *Institutes*, III.xx.31

47. Calvin, *Institutes*, III.xx.33.

48. Calvin, *Genevan Confession of Faith* (1536), CTT, 30–31.

49. Calvin, *Institutes*, IV.x.31.

50. Calvin, *Shunning the Unlawful Rites* (1537), *Selected Works* 3:379.

of images, the receiving of extreme unction, the purchase of indulgences, and the sprinkling of water."[51]

Like other Reformers of the sixteenth century, Calvin denounces those abuses that involved ritual. The two main errors of the church under the papacy were (1) the retention of rituals that were useless and absurd, and (2) the multiplicity of rituals. Having many rituals, he says, is oppressive to the conscience of people (i.e., because they are thought to be necessary for salvation), such that people cling to them rather than to Christ himself. One reason for the ritual overloading of the church, Calvin opines, is that we humans like things of our own invention because we can see ourselves in them, meaning that ritual can become a form of self-flattery. Furthermore, rituals can give the false appearance of training people in humility, when in fact they are no more than bodily exercises.[52] While people are captivated by rituals, these are really empty displays that were actually inspired by pagan thinking and practice and by Mosaic ceremonial law, which no longer applies to Christians.

Rather than edifying Christians, many rituals merely "stupefy" them.[53] By handing down numerous ceremonial commands and prohibitions with increasing harshness, church leaders have made the lives of Christians harsh and unbearable.[54] Moreover, the burdensome number of rituals has effectively buried Christ and nearly returned the church to Judaism. Calvin rejects the argument that the weak in faith need rituals, arguing that Christians should not be overwhelmed with numerous rituals. While God trained ancient peoples by signs and figures (i.e., ceremonies), God desired to provide Christians with a simpler training based less on external things. This distinction between God's modus operandi with the people of the old versus the new covenants finds its basis in John 4:23 ("But a time is coming and has now come when the true worshipers will worship the Father in spirit and in truth, for the Father is seeking such as these to worship Him"). Under the old covenant, Calvin says, the spiritual worship of God was only foreshadowed, and unfortunately, was obscured by the multiplicity of ceremonies which have been abolished under the new covenant. To confound this distinction is to subvert the very order that has been established by Christ himself.[55]

---

51. Calvin, *Shunning the Unlawful Rites, Selected Works* 3:379.

52. Calvin, *Institutes*, IV.x.11.

53. Calvin, *Institutes*, IV.x.12.

54. Calvin, *Institutes*, IV.x.13.

55. Calvin, *Institutes*, IV.x.14.

This does not mean, however, that the church should refrain from providing ceremonies to help the ignorant and weak in faith. But Calvin contends that rituals should not obscure Christ and that there should be a moderate use of rituals marked by "fewness in number, facility in observance, and significancy of meaning which consists in clearness."[56]

As for the sacraments, Calvin defines a sacrament as "an outward sign by which the Lord seals on our consciences the promises of his good will toward us in order to sustain the weakness of our faith; and we in turn attest our piety toward him in the presence of the Lord and of his angels and before [humanity]."[57] The outward signs are added to the promises as a way of confirming them—meaning that the sacraments are meant to evoke and strengthen faith in God's promises. Thus, a sacrament consists of both the word and the external sign (i.e., the sacramental element). Calvin emphasizes that the "word," in this case, is the preached word, spoken aloud by the minister, which (1) leads us to the reality signified in the sacrament, and (2) clarifies the meaning of the visible sign.[58] Calvin thus draws not only on Augustine's teaching that a sacrament equals word plus element, but also the Augustinian understanding that the efficacy of sacraments rests on a faith that believes the word.[59]

As for the number of sacraments, Calvin identifies only baptism and the Lord's Supper as sacraments.[60] He notes that while theologians in the early church called many rites and ceremonies "sacraments," they only speak of baptism and the Lord's Supper as things which testify to God's grace. He references Augustine's teaching that Christ linked his church together by only a few sacraments, namely, baptism and the Supper.[61] The other five traditional sacraments—confirmation, penance, marriage, ordination, and extreme unction (anointing of the dying)—are referred to by Calvin as "ceremonies."[62]

Calvin offers two significant qualifications concerning the sacraments. First, he states that the sacramental elements (water, bread, wine) do not possess spiritual qualities by their own nature, but rather because they have been

56. Calvin, *Institutes*, IV.x.14.

57. Calvin, *Institutes*, IV.xiv.1.

58. Calvin, *Institutes*, IV.xiv.4.

59. Calvin, *Institutes*, IV.xiv.4.

60. Calvin, *Institutes*, IV.xiv.20; IV.xix.3.

61. Calvin, *Institutes*, IV.xix.3.

62. Calvin, *Institutes*, IV.xix.4–37.

designated by God for the purpose of representing spiritual things.[63] Second, the sacraments do not justify or confer grace on recipients in their own right (provided that the recipient has not engaged in mortal sin), as traditional teaching held. Such an understanding, in Calvin's view, promises righteousness apart from faith, gives rise to a superstitious focus on earthly things rather than on God, presumes to offer more than is promised by the Word of God and is obtained by faith, and suggests that mere participation in the sacraments justifies, when in fact justification is in Christ alone. On this matter he points to Augustine's teaching that there can be "invisible sanctification without the visible sign, and a visible sign without true sanctification."[64] The function of the sacraments, like the preaching of the Word, is to offer Christ, but they are of no benefit unless received by faith. Yet the sacraments are not comparable to "grace being poured into a cup," since they only serve to "testify and confirm" that grace toward us.

But if faith is required for the sacraments, how can Calvin say that the sacraments are given for the confirmation of faith (as in the definition above)? His answer is that there is only a beginning of faith in every Christian that needs to be constantly nourished. This need for the confirmation (strengthening) of one's faith does not imply a lack of faith, but a recognition that Christians will have to struggle against doubt or a lack of trust in God throughout their lives.[65]

Indeed, the sacraments for Calvin are a kind of a divine accommodation to limited human capabilities. Because our corporeal nature makes it difficult for us to understand spiritual things,

> our merciful Lord, according to his infinite kindness, so tempers himself to our capacity that, since we are creatures who always creep on the ground, cleave to the flesh, and, do not think about or even conceive of anything spiritual, he condescends to lead us to himself even by these earthly elements, and to set before us in the flesh a mirror of spiritual blessings.[66]

Insofar as the sacraments are "aids to our necessity," we cannot do without them. To consistently abstain from the sacrament (i.e., the Lord's

---

63. Calvin, *Institutes*, IV.xiv.3
64. Calvin, *Institutes*, IV.xiv.14.
65. Calvin, *Catechism of the Church of Geneva* (1545), *CTT*, 132.
66. Calvin, *Institutes*, IV.xiv.3.

Supper) is to show contempt for Christ and his grace, and to thwart the work of the Holy Spirit.[67]

Distinctive in Calvin's sacramental theology is the role that he accords to the Holy Spirit. No benefit from the sacrament is received unless the Holy Spirit is present to open a person's heart and mind to what is promised in the sacrament.[68] The sacraments, however, do not impart the Holy Spirit to every participant, but only to those whom God desires to give the Holy Spirit, who in turn causes the recipient to receive the sacrament by faith and to bring forth the proper fruits of the sacrament. Thus, although the Spirit is at work in the sacrament, there is still a difference between the internal grace of the Spirit and the external ministry.[69] But if the Holy Spirit seals the promise on the mind, how can the action be attributable to the sacrament? Calvin's answer is that while the role of the Holy Spirit is "to move and affect the heart, to illumine the mind and to render the conscience pure and tranquil," the sacrament serves as a "secondary means" in the process.[70] Even though it is God's intention to use the sacraments as instruments, this does not detract from the power and efficacy of the Holy Spirit.

Accordingly, a sacrament is not necessarily efficacious (capable of producing an effect) for every recipient. While Calvin can say that a sacrament truly does what it promises,[71] this understanding is nevertheless qualified by his doctrine of election. Noting that for Calvin the outward sign of baptism is not necessarily contemporaneous with its internal effect, liturgical scholar Maxwell Johnson concludes that baptism is efficacious only for the elect in Calvin's theology. In other words, baptism truly does what it promises (effects what it signifies) only for those predestined for salvation by God. For all others, neither baptism nor anything else will change one's standing before God. Since the truly elect in the church are known only to God, all must be baptized and remain loyal church members.[72]

The primary abuse with respect to the sacraments, according to Calvin, is that they have been overloaded with rituals that obscure their true meaning. While the baptism established by Jesus and observed by the disciples was simple, later generations added "chrism, salt, spittle, and tapers."

---

67. Calvin, *Catechism of Geneva*, *CTT*, 132.

68. Calvin, *Institutes*, IV.xiv.17.

69. Calvin, *Institutes*, IV.xiv.17.

70. Calvin, *Catechism of Geneva*, *CTT*, 131.

71. Calvin, *Institutes*, IV.xiv.17.

72. Johnson, *Rites of Christian Initiation*, 337.

Schoolmen and preachers then "extolled the efficacy of these [secondary] signs, rather than pointing to Christ."[73] Regarding the Supper he writes:

> The devil introduced the manner of celebrating the Supper without any doctrine, and in place of doctrine substituted ceremonies, partly unfitting and useless, and partly even dangerous, from which much ill has followed—to such an extent, that the mass, which takes the place of the Supper in the popish church, when strictly defined, is nothing but pure apishness and buffoonery.[74]

He complains that since the priest conducts the mass using a very low voice, the mystery is not explained to the people nor the promises articulated in their hearing. It would appear, then, that for Calvin, a sacramental ritual must be carefully linked to the sacred story upon which it is based. Elsewhere, he bolsters the case for the need to expound the meaning of the sacraments by stating the following:

> We have recalled the ancient custom that the administration of the sacraments be accompanied by doctrine, expounding with all diligence and fidelity both their advantages and their legitimate use. . . . Nothing is more alien to the nature of the sacrament than to set before the people an empty spectacle, unaccompanied with explanation of the mystery. There is the well-known passage, quoted by Gratian from Augustine: "If the word is wanting, the water is nothing but an element." What he means by "word" he immediately explains when he says, "That is, the word of faith which we preach."[75]

By way of summary, we highlight the following themes in John Calvin's teaching on ritual and the sacraments:

1. Obedience. Since the Word is the revelation of God's sovereign will to humanity, for Calvin it is the supreme determinant of Christian life and worship. Accordingly, the individual Christian and the church are obligated to obey God's Word when it comes to ritual matters. But there is nevertheless a certain amount of nuance in Calvin when it comes to the matter of obedience. Calvin could allow the use of gestures not explicitly enjoined by Scripture, but which nevertheless reflected the practices of the apostles and early church. He also recognized that a church's context had a role in determining which

---

73. Calvin, *Necessity of Reforming the Church* (1539), *CTT*, 203.

74. Calvin, *Treatise on the Lord's Supper* (1541), *CTT*, 161.

75. Calvin, *Necessity of Reforming the Church*, *CTT*, 203.

rituals to use and which to discard. On ritual, Calvin was biblical without being biblicist.

2. Freedom. Like other Reformers, Calvin insisted that churches should not be compelled to engage in rituals that are not necessary for salvation. Such compulsion placed an undue burden on the conscience. Instead, Christians should use rituals with sincerity and faith, thereby living out their evangelical freedom. Because ritual practice is a matter of freedom, churches may change or discard rituals as necessary. However, freedom does not mean that Christians should despise rituals and ceremony, especially those that lend order and decorum to church life. Freedom in Calvin's mind is circumscribed by a love that seeks the good of the church.

3. Edification. For Calvin, rituals are not practiced for their own sake or merely to meet a psychological need for ritual. Rather, ritual is to lead Christians to God, and thereby build up the church in faith and love. For Calvin, ritual is part of the church's whole ministry of the Word whose goal is the formation of Christians who are knowledgeable and mature in the faith. Ministry cannot to be reduced to mindless ritualizing.

4. Simplicity. Frequently, Calvin complains that too many rituals hamper Christian life and worship, especially the sacraments. This multiplicity of rituals served only to burden Christians with actions that are not edifying and ultimately distract from the true worship of God. Accordingly, Calvin discarded practices that he viewed as inimical to his goals of edification and freedom, and endeavored to simplify baptism and the Lord's Supper, whose biblical descriptions are at wide variance from the ritual-heavy rites of the Roman Catholic Church of his time.

Comparing and Contrasting Luther and Calvin on Ritual and the Sacraments

Although there is a tendency to emphasize the theological differences between Luther and Calvin, it is clear that their thinking about ritual is similar in certain ways. Both recognized that ritual has a legitimate role in church life, not only for the sake of good ecclesiastical order but also for the spiritual formation of Christians. Accordingly, they were critical of those who despised rituals. While viewing ritual as necessary for the church's existence, both distinguished between "necessary for order" and "necessary for salvation," and so advocated freedom in the use of ritual, in the sense that churches should never feel compelled to engage in rituals that lack a clear divine command. With the idea of freedom in mind, both argued that rituals could be dropped, added, or modified according to a church's circumstances. Luther and Calvin were also united in espousing ritual simplicity, in the sense that Christians should not have to endure an overwhelming number of rituals in their public and private worship. Finally, both taught that Old Testament rituals were irrelevant for Christians because the death and resurrection of Jesus Christ established a new covenant.[76]

Perhaps the most notable difference between Luther and Calvin concerns the degree to which the church is free in ritual matters. In his baptismal rite, Calvin is adamant that there can be no opting for any practice that lacks either a divine command or an example of apostolic usage.[77] But for Luther, actions and practices not specifically commanded were left free, that is, to the discretion of the church. It was for this reason that he eschewed the forceful removal and violent destruction of sacred art ("images"), whose retention might be helpful to some Christians. It seems that Calvin was less willing than Luther to accommodate the "weak in faith."

We also see significant differences between Luther and Calvin on the sacraments. For Luther the sacraments confer divine grace, that is, they give to the believing recipient the saving benefits of Jesus' death and resurrection at the very time of their conferral. By contrast, Calvin viewed the sacraments as only signifying this grace, meaning that the benefits are not automatically conferred when they are received. While Calvin essentially held that the sacraments benefit only the elect (those persons predestined to salvation), Luther does not bring election into his sacramental theology. In contrast to Luther's downplaying the idea that the sacraments are identity markers, Calvin accords the idea some importance, especially in his definition of the sacraments. Finally, while communion with the body and blood of Christ

---

76. Admittedly, both Luther and Calvin tended to view the new covenant as superceding the old covenant and the church as replacing Israel as the new or true people of God. While such views have grounding in the New Testament (Eph 2; Heb 8:6), Christians today should not allow supersessionist theology to become a basis for denigrating the Jewish religion or despising the Jewish people. Counterbalancing supersessionist thinking is Paul's view that God has not rejected his people Israel and will ultimately have mercy on them (Rom 11:1, 31).

77. Calvin, "Form of Administering the Sacraments (Baptism)," *Selected Works* 2:118.

is for both Reformers the benefit of the Lord's Supper, for Luther this communion is based on Jesus' own promise ("This is my body,"/"This cup is the New Testament in my blood"), while for Calvin it is due to the work of the Holy Spirit, who enables the participant to ascend to heaven in spirit and experience communion with the risen and ascended Christ there.

Despite significant differences in their sacramental theologies, Luther and Calvin did share a few similarities on the sacraments. Both viewed the sacraments as representing a divine accommodation to human capacities and weakness. A concern that ritual embellishments not overwhelm the rites of baptism and the Lord's Supper was held by both. Finally, Augustine's emphasis on a faith-filled reception of the sacraments is a common theme in the writings of both Reformers.

Conclusion

This chapter has described and analyzed the thoughts of two great Reformers on ritual. But can we take their teachings seriously today? Are they relevant for us as we think about the place of ritual in the contemporary church's liturgy? While it is true that our world is vastly different from Europe in the early sixteenth century, I believe that what Luther and Calvin say about ritual is relevant for us because their teachings are grounded in the Scriptures and the early church fathers, and thus they are catholic in their outlook—attentive to what has been believed, taught, and confessed by churches at all times and in all places. They were not narrow, idiosyncratic, or parochial, and thus can speak to Christian communities well beyond their own milieu. But they were also evangelical—desirous of bringing about renewal grounded in the good news of Jesus. As voices at once catholic and evangelical, Luther and Calvin embody what all theologians and serious Christian thinkers should be. In that case, we must take seriously their reflections on ritual as we develop our own understanding about ritual in Christian worship. Their insights will now serve as the groundwork for this book's final chapter, a guide to ritual in Christian worship.

Chapter 6

Ritual Principles

Introduction

IN REGARD TO RITUAL, this book has offered definitions, examined certain life science views, discussed different components, surveyed the Bible, and explored the teachings of Martin Luther and John Calvin on the matter. My purpose has been to help the reader understand the role of ritual in Christian worship, and to develop a theological-historical perspective on ritual. I conclude this volume by offering several ritual principles that emerge from the previous discussions, particularly the chapter on Luther and Calvin. I hope that these can serve as a guide for liturgical practice and enable worship leaders to think critically about ritual. Yet I recognize that every context is different: some churches elaborate their public worship services with numerous gestures, symbols, and ceremonies, while others are restrained in their use of ceremony. Accordingly, these principles are meant to be general enough so that they can speak to a variety of contexts, but not so broad that they fail to speak meaningfully.

Ritual Serves the Gospel

Ritual in Christian public worship proclaims the good news of Jesus crucified and raised from the dead, and enables Christians to appropriate that reality. The New Testament gospels indicate that the mission of the church is not only to share the story of Jesus' saving deeds (Matt 28:18–20; Mark 16:15; Luke 24:45–49), but also to enact that story by baptizing, sharing a supper in memory of him, and by absolving sinners in response to his post-resurrection command (John 20:21–23). Other ritual acts in the New Testament relate to the Jesus story by (1) sharing it verbally (ritual song);

(2) setting apart ministers to publicly proclaim it (ordination); (3) signifying its life-giving dimensions (anointing for healing; Jas 5:13–16); and (4) praying for its promised benefits (Matt 6:9–13; 1 Tim 2:1–2), whether in public worship or private devotions. Both Luther and Calvin were aware, however, that ritual could serve purposes that are inimical to the gospel, for example, to heighten the importance and holiness of clergy through elaborate ordination gestures.

Today churches need to exercise care so that life-cycle rituals in particular do not stress the human story at the expense of God's story. The Christian ritualization of death must be more than a matter of paying tributes to those who have died in the Lord. A wake with personal reminiscences about the deceased and the displaying of objects associated with him/her (cf. Acts 9:39) is rightly followed by a funeral that tells the story of Jesus' resurrection and uses rituals objects that point to his resurrection victory, e.g., a pall to cover the (closed) casket and a paschal candle placed near the casket. Similarly, the marriage service of Christians needs to be more than a celebration of the couple's individual personalities and mutual relationship. While the officiating clergyperson at a wedding may share the story of the couple's journey toward marriage, the story of Jesus the Bridegroom is fittingly proclaimed not only in the wedding sermon but also in a nuptial celebration of the Lord's Supper—a foretaste of the marriage Supper of the Lamb. Far from being mere liturgical trappings, rituals and sacraments can offer the comfort and assurance of the gospel to those experiencing anxiety in times of transition.

Ritual Serves Freedom

Ritual arises out of a sense of joy, freedom, and anticipation, rather than compulsion. Christians should not feel compelled to observe particular rituals—nor to abstain from them. Some actions, of course, are essential for the appropriation of the gospel (e.g., preaching, baptizing, celebrating the Lord's Supper) because these are bound up with the very presence of the Lord Jesus himself. Hence, they are nonnegotiable.

But even with these there is room for variation; some aspects of the sacraments are not biblically mandated and can be left to the discretion of the local church, e.g., whether to use red versus white wine, or wafers versus a loaf of bread at the Lord's Supper. Similarly, baptism may be administered through the pouring of water or by immersing the candidate completely in a large pool of water. Baptism may be elaborated by the presentation of a candle and/or the clothing of the newly baptized in white garments. Or, alternatively, we may not do these things. Sacred art and various crafted symbols of wood, metal, stone, or fabric may or may not adorn our liturgical spaces. Elaborations to the sacramental rites and to the liturgical space will depend on the sensibilities and sensitivities of the local church community.

Yet, while some ritual matters are of a secondary nature and thus discretionary, this does not mean that they are unimportant and need not be considered. To the contrary, we recognize that secondary rituals can speak the gospel and draw people into participation by appealing to the senses and involving the entire body. Rather than using our "freedom" in ritual matters as an excuse for indifference, we ought to ask how we may use it to serve both the gospel and the church community.

Ritual Serves Good Order[1]

Ritual gives order, direction, purpose, and substance to the church, such that it can maintain its existence as a spiritual institution. Liturgical orders with their patterned structures (gathering, Word, meal, and sending) enable weekly public worship to be consistently focused on those actions that are central to the life and mission of the church, namely, the proclamation of God's Word and the celebration of the sacraments. Set times for the church's public liturgy allow Word and sacrament to be part of the rhythm of personal prayer and devotion as Christians live and work in the world.

More than just a convenient central location for public services, appointed liturgical spaces provide an environment that continually shapes a community's spirituality through the arrangement of its liturgical centers (pulpit, font, table) and other symbols that express the community's faith. The rhythm of the liturgical calendar (the "church year") maintains a focus on the church's central beliefs about its Lord and Redeemer, and the customary rituals for the various yearly celebrations (e.g., the imposition of ashes on Ash Wednesday, the striking of a new fire and candle procession at the Easter Vigil) enable Christians to participate in the mystery of Christ through bodily movement. The repertoire of songs sung throughout the year imprint theological truths on the mind, insofar as the metered verse and rhyme of song texts make theological ideas memorable. Because all of these ritual structures work together to provide order, focus,

---

1. 1 Cor 14:40.

and predictability, discerning worship leaders are cautious about changing them unnecessarily and thoughtlessly.

Ritual Serves Unity

Rather than leading to division in the church, ritual unites. Churches believe that they are united in a mystical fellowship not only because they believe the same things, but because they do the same things: preach the Word, baptize, and gather for a meal that proclaims Jesus' death and resurrection—all ritual acts. In other words, the universal church finds communion in these "holy things" (sacramental rituals) that enable it to be "in Christ."

Yet culture, history, and distinctive theological emphases have given rise to numerous ceremonial variations in the sacramental rites of churches, such that ministers of one tradition might offer a full prayer of thanksgiving over the bread and cup at the Lord's Supper, while those of another tradition might bless ("consecrate") the bread and cup by simply sharing the story of Jesus' final meal with his disciples, i.e., by reciting the Words of Institution.

The universal church also knows of a variety of distinctive rituals and customs that surround the holy things: e.g., the use of candles, vestments, or a common ecumenical lectionary. However, churches avoid strife and division over these secondary ritual matters. They follow the ancient church's dictum that "differences over fasting do not violate the unity of the church," believing that true unity is grounded in the Lord Jesus himself. Yet agreement in nonessential ritual matters is not rejected. We might note how Luther commended agreement in voluntary "external matters" (i.e., "ceremonies"), since, in his view, this concord promoted peace and harmony in the church and helped to commend the church to the world. Indeed, such agreement on ritual matters serves mission and evangelism, since ceremonial variations pose a potential stumbling block to seekers and unchurched persons. The recent ecumenical trend toward the adoption of a fourfold service order consisting of gathering, Word, meal, and sending and the use of a common lectionary are therefore welcome developments. Continued efforts to share liturgical rituals and customs would ultimately help to enrich the church and present a much-needed image of unity to the world.

Ritual Serves Clarity

Ritual is used in a way that allows the central aspects of a rite to remain central. As noted previously, one of the chief criticisms of the sixteenth-century Reformers was that the church's liturgies were overloaded with rituals. Moreover, many rituals seemed irrelevant and absurd (e.g., anointing bells and altars), and placed a heavy burden on the clergy and people who were expected to lead and participate in them. The critiques of Luther and Calvin helped the church to identify which ritual acts are the most central to the rites of baptism and the Lord's Supper.

Luther, for example, cleared away the ritual overgrowth in baptism and thereby highlighted the central importance of the baptismal washing—which he thought should be administered by immersion! Yet, while Luther downgraded confirmation from a sacrament to a churchly rite of blessing involving no more than a laying on of hands,[2] later Lutherans developed a rite of confirmation embellished with catechetical questions and answers, handshakes, bell tolls, and other gestures. We might wonder whether a highly ritualized confirmation like this goes well beyond Luther's intentions and perhaps overshadows baptism in importance. Accordingly, a restrained confirmation rite would enable baptism to be perceived as the premier rite of Christian initiation.

Admittedly, however, baptism is so rich and multifaceted in meaning that "secondary" or "explanatory" rituals are perhaps needed to express this richness. Arguably, baptism deserves a ritual anointing to express the "anointing of the Holy Spirit" (Acts 2:38; 1 John 2:20, 27), and also the conferral of a ritual garment to portray the idea of being "clothed with Christ" in baptism (Gal 3:27). Indeed, because baptism has traditionally been conferred on naked or partially naked bodies, a ritual clothing of that body is by no means unimportant. Nevertheless, these additional rituals should be discretionary—governed by "may" rubrics. Of course, leaders are wise to introduce (or eliminate) elaborative features cautiously.

The need for ritual clarity does not preclude a fullness of ritual expression. Because the center of Holy Communion is the giving of thanks and the eating and drinking of bread and wine, a loaf of freshly baked bread is used and all may drink from a large ceremonial cup, in line with 1 Corinthians 10:16. Baptism aptly involves a full dunking in water in order to

---

2. Luther, *Babylonian Captivity*, AL 3:96. See also Luther, *Predigt am Sonntag Lätare Nachmittages* ("Sermon for Laetare Afternoon"), March 15, 1523, WA 11, 66.

enact one's baptismal death and resurrection (Rom 6) and the washing of regeneration in the Holy Spirit (Titus 3); otherwise, the application of water should get the candidate's head and upper body thoroughly wet. While it is true that our doing more does not mean that God will grant grace more abundantly, ritual reductionism hardly edifies the assembly. How, after all, can we appreciate the idea that baptism is a washing if the application of water is no more than the placing of a wet hand on a person's head? How is communion a Supper or meal when it consists of drinking miniscule amounts of wine and eating thin wafers that bear no resemblance to actual bread? Simplicity cannot be an excuse for minimalism.

Ritual Serves Relevance

Rituals are relevant both theologically (biblically) and culturally. Because ritual forms thinking, believing, and living that is consistent with a faith community's teaching, rituals speak biblical-theological truth in ways that are relevant to the participants. Many ritual acts and symbols endure over time not only because they express the church's core teachings, but also because they resonate with the realities of human life. Eating and bathing are essential aspects of life, and so baptism and the Lord's Supper are the ritual-sacramental core of public worship in most Christian churches. While life and faith join together meaningfully in baptism and the Lord's Supper, such has not been the case for all rituals in the church's vast repertoire.

Even though exorcism is mentioned in the New Testament, it seems mostly irrelevant in modern Western cultures—although African and Asian churches continue to practice it. Rituals with less direct or no biblical grounding are open to criticism when they are at odds with culture. Some Christians might question the validity of ringing bells and lighting candles when there is little need nowadays to summon people to church (the original purpose of bells) or to provide extra lighting for a minister to read a liturgical book (the original purpose of candles). Certainly, churches may not want to undertake a ritual house cleaning that could prove disturbing to some church members. But they may also want to avoid introducing new rituals that will not endure beyond their current cultural context or which seem to lack any solid biblical or theological grounding.

Ritual Serves Faith Formation

Sacraments and rituals form and build up the faith of Christians. As Hwarang Moon points out, "Experience is inscribed in the body, and through the participation of the body, is inscribed in the memory."[3] Thomas Groome likewise argues that memory comes through bodily experience and, furthermore, that the body itself stores memories.[4] The role of ritual in faith formation, in fact, has long been appreciated. In the Old Testament, the Passover enabled Jewish families to pass on the memories and faith of Israel to succeeding generations, and children were expected to question their elders about the meaning of the feast (Exod 12:26). The formative character of ritual was also appreciated by the Reformers. Calvin viewed ritual as a means of "disciplining" the faith of Christians for the sake of "doctrine, discipline, and the sacraments."[5] Similarly, Luther valued the role of "ceremonies" in forming young people, namely, by helping them to gain a sound understanding of the Christian faith. But for Luther ritual does more than inculcate correct knowledge; it allows participants to experience the presence of God in a personal way, or in his words, to "feel God with [one's] hands."

Because ritual forms faith and understanding, churches may want to work toward greater inclusion of children and the intellectually challenged in their worship services. If spiritual truth can be appropriated by both the mind and the body, then worship services should include persons at all levels of cognitive ability. We may want to rethink the practice of dismissing children from the worship service (or not having them in the service at all), and reconsider the traditional belief that the cognitively challenged do not belong in Christian worship. Both groups learn through their bodies, which can experience sights, sounds, and tastes, and they can engage in simple gestures such as making the sign of the cross on themselves. These experiences in Christian worship can also form children and the cognitively challenged in the beliefs and affections of the Christian community.[6]

---

3. Moon, *Engraved Upon the Heart*, 149.

4. See Groome, *Educating for Life*, 106. Cited in Moon, *Engraved Upon the Heart*, 149.

5. Calvin, "Reply to Sadolet," 232. Cited in Moon, *Engraved Upon the Heart*, 32.

6. See Moon, *Engraved Upon the Heart*, chapter 5.

Ritual Serves Participation

Rituals invite the participation of the liturgical assembly. Far more than an audience that passively observes the ritual activities of worship leaders, members of the liturgical assembly are ritual co-actors with the leaders. Thus, it is important for the assembly to participate as actively as possible in ritual. Specifically, their *bodies* need to be active in rituals. Passive ritual participation cannot be expected to adequately form people. In addition to hearing and seeing, the senses of touch and taste need to be utilized. This would mean, for example, a more regular if not weekly celebration of the Lord's Supper. If regular meals are needed to nourish bodies depleted by work, then regular communion with the Lord Jesus is needed to replenish spirits depleted by the struggle to maintain belief in God and love for the neighbor.

Maximizing assembly participation in baptism is especially desirable. We need to understand that baptism is the church's rite of initiation, not the family's. If a church regularly administers baptism outside of the Sunday service, it might consider scheduling at least some baptisms during the Sunday service so that assembly members are reminded of their own baptism. The entire assembly can be asked to gather around the font, and if that is not possible, younger children can be gathered about the font so that they get a better view of the ritual action. As suggested previously, the baptismal candidates might be fully immersed so that they come to appreciate both intellectually and bodily how baptism encompasses their entire lives.

Finally, while the participation of assembly members at funerals has traditionally been limited to seeing and hearing, some ritual gestures might be used at funerals in order to enhance participation. Following the lowering of the coffin into the grave, mourners might toss fresh-cut flowers (symbols of life and paradise) into the grave as a way of commending the deceased to God's care. Likewise, to maximize bodily participation, assembly members might be invited to shovel token amounts of soil onto the casket as a way of helping to prepare the deceased for the next phase of his/her baptismal journey.[7]

---

7. I note the custom in Japanese churches whereby mourners present flowers to the memory of the deceased as part of the funeral service itself.

Ritual Serves Love

Ritual is used in loving regard for our Christian brothers and sisters. In other words, the way that ritual is used considers the sensitivities and capabilities of all assembly members. This means, first of all, that rituals are not introduced or withdrawn so as to trouble or offend fellow Christians, that is, capriciously and without providing an explanation for the change. We noted earlier in this work how Luther opposed the forceful removal of sacred art from churches, questioning whether this iconoclasm exemplified Christian love. In the North American context today, worship leaders might want to resist the urge to remove symbols that may seem inappropriate or outdated (e.g., national flags), recognizing that such action may offend those with strong patriotic feelings. Second, this principle also dictates that rituals are suited to the abilities of assembly members. So, for example, assembly songs are to be appropriate for those with minimal musical training, e.g., by having only a few note values, few or no rests, and a range within an octave (the eight notes of the musical scale). More difficult songs are given to trained singers (soloists, choir members). Although such songs often have greater musical interest, accommodating the less musically trained members of the assembly with simpler songs ensures greater participation by these persons and communicates a greater sense of inclusion and welcome into the church community.

Ritual Serves Hospitality

Ritual makes public worship welcoming to the participants. Churches are mindful that seekers and others with little experience in Christian worship may be overwhelmed and baffled by the rituals, gestures, ceremonial structures, and symbols of Christian worship. Accordingly, rituals are "few in number" (to use Calvin's phrase). Worship leaders avoid the urge to constantly create new rituals and to over-embellish the sacramental rites.

Those actions that form the core ritual repertoire are led with confidence by leaders who understand their history and theology and are able to explain them to the assembly. Indeed, worship leaders provide ritual formation for the community in the various educational programs of the church (e.g., baptismal preparation, confirmation, new member instruction, etc.). If the principles of clarity (having few rituals), meaning, and engagement described above are enacted, and worship leaders provide sound teaching about ritual, seekers are more likely to find the assembly's liturgy inviting.

At the same time the needs of established church members are not neglected. Ritual stability and consistency enable experienced Christians to continue feeling "at home" in the liturgy, such that they can consistently appropriate the theological content of ritual and grow spiritually. Hence the principles related to the gospel and good order above are crucial for long-time church members. Vitally important for all church members is the understanding that ritual *serves* the assembly and God, as opposed to the whims or personal agendas of worship leaders. Christians will see that the idea of service is already embedded to some extent in our working definition of ritual, insofar as ritual has to do with forming people in the ways and beliefs of a faith community. If formation is the goal of ritual, then the needs of participants will always be considered and worship rituals will always have an inviting character.

Conclusion

The assumption of this chapter is that while ritual is part of who we are, we can nevertheless reflect on our ritual acts, make judgments about them, and change or modify them when necessary. We are not bound to our rituals absolutely. But we cannot do without ritual, since customs and habits help us to manage life, and because ritual is a necessity for embodied creatures like ourselves. We are not just minds who happen to be in bodies, rather, our minds are embodied.

Ritual forms our hearts and minds through the bodies that mediate the world to us. We learn about the world and about God's redemptive works through the senses of hearing and seeing, but also through touch, taste, and smell (baptism, the Lord's Supper), by which we increase our perception of our surroundings (getting close to the actions). Similarly, we learn through gestures that symbolize aspects of the gospel (e.g., making the sign of the cross at the mention of the Holy Trinity, raising and waving hands during the song set of a contemporary worship service). Ritual is performed with the whole body and encompasses the whole self. To think that ritual is an aspect of Christian life and devotion that can be easily jettisoned is shortsighted and contrary to the wisdom of Christians throughout the ages.

We could say, therefore, that ritual is "catholic"—it has been part of church life wherever and whenever the church has existed. Furthermore, some ritual acts are for all churches everywhere, in particular, those that ground the church in the gospel. Alongside the catholicity of ritual, there exists an evangelical spirit that calls Christians to ask whether their rituals are truly serving the gospel. That spirit was at work in Martin Luther and John Calvin, who, while appreciative of the role played by ritual and ceremony in Christian worship, nevertheless asked critical questions about rituals in light of the gospel. We can do nothing better than to be evangelical-catholics like them in our use and evaluation of ritual!

Bibliography

Anderson, Paul N. "Quaker Worship." In *DLW*, 394–97.

Apostolic Constitutions. Edited by James Donaldson. In *The Ante-Nicene Fathers: Translations of the Writings of the Fathers Down to A.D. 325*, edited by Alexander Roberts, James Donaldson, et al., 7:391–505. Edinburgh: T. & T. Clark, 1886. Reprinted Grand Rapids: Eerdmans, 1989.

Bailey, Regina. "How Colors Affect Human Behavior." *ThoughtCo.*, June 2020. https://www.thoughtco.com/color-psychology-and-human-behavior-4151666.

The Book of Common Prayer and Administration of the Sacraments and Other Rites and Ceremonies of the Church. New York: Seabury, 1979.

The Book of Common Prayer: The Texts of 1549, 1559, and 1662. Edited by Brian Cummings. Oxford: Oxford University Press, 2011.

Book of Common Worship. Louisville: Westminster John Knox, 1993.

The Book of Concord. Edited by Robert Kolb and Timothy J. Wengert. Minneapolis: Fortress, 2000.

Bradshaw, Paul F. "Daily Prayer." In *DLW*, 140–41.

Bradshaw, Paul F., and Maxwell E. Johnson. *The Origins of Feasts, Fasts and Seasons in Early Christianity*. Alcuin Club Collections 86. Collegeville, MN: Liturgical, 2011.

Brugh, Lorraine, S., and Gordon W. Lathrop. *The Sunday Assembly*. Vol. 1 of Using Evangelical Lutheran Worship. Minneapolis: Augsburg Fortress, 2008.

Caemmerer, Richard. *Preaching for the Church*. St. Louis: Concordia, 1959.

Calvin, John. *Calvin: Theological Treatises*. Edited and translated by J. K. S. Reid. Vol. 22 of Library of Christian Classics. Louisville: Westminster John Knox, 2006.

———. *Commentary on the Acts of the Apostles 1–13*. Translated by John W. Fraser and W. J. G. McDonald. Calvin's Commentaries. Edinburgh: St Andrew, 1965.

———. *Institutes of the Christian Religion* (1559). 2 vols. Vol. 20 of Library of Christian Classics. Edited by John T. McNeill. Translated by Ford Lewis Battles. Philadelphia: Westminster, 1960.

———. *Selected Works of John Calvin: Tracts and Letters*. Edited by Henry Beveridge and Jules Bonnet. 6 vols. Grand Rapids: Baker, 1983.

Costen, Melva Wilson. "Black Churches' Worship (USA)." In *DLW*, 62–64.

Constitution on the Sacred Liturgy. Washington, DC: United States Catholic Conference, 1995.

Daniels, Marilyn. *The Dance in Christianity: A History of Religious Dance Through the Ages*. New York: Paulist, 1981.

Davies, J. G. *Liturgical Dance: An Historical, Theological and Practical Handbook*. London: SCM, 1984.

Dawtry, Anne. "Art and Worship." In *DLW*, 28–29.

Eliade, Mircea. *Rites and Symbols of Initiation: The Mysteries of Birth and Rebirth*. Translated by Willard R. Trask. Woodstock, CT: Spring, 1995.

———. *The Sacred and the Profane: The Nature of Religion*. Translated by Willard R. Trask. New York: Harcourt Brace, 1987.

Evangelical Lutheran Church in America. *Principles for Worship*. Minneapolis: Augsburg Fortress, 2002.

———. *Use of the Means of Grace: A Statement on the Practice of Word and Sacrament*. Minneapolis: Augsburg Fortress, 1997.

Evangelical Lutheran Worship (Pew Edition). Minneapolis: Augsburg Fortress, 2006.

Feinberg, C. L. "Synagogue." In *NBD*, 1142–43.

Freeman, D. "Purim." In *NBD*, 991.

———. "Sabbatical Year." In *NBD*, 1033.

———. "Showbread." In *NBD*, 1098.

Galley, Howard E. *The Ceremonies of the Eucharist: A Guide to Celebration*. Cambridge, MA: Cowley, 1989.

Gaventa, Beverley Roberts. *The Acts of the Apostles*. Abingdon New Testament Commentaries. Nashville, TN: Abingdon, 2003.

Gehman, Henry. "Blood." In *WDB*, 121.

———. "Burial." In *WDB*, 129.

———. "Candlestick." In *WDB*, 142.

———. "Circumcision." In *WDB*, 176–77.

———. "Feast." In *WDB*, 296.

———. "Jubilee." In *WDB*, 521–22.

———. "Marriage." In *WDB*, 590–92.

———. "Mourning." In *WDB*, 640.

———. "Purim." In *WDB*, 782.

———. "Sepulcher." In *WDB*, 848–49.

———. "Showbread." In *WDB*, 876–77.

———. "Synagogue." In *WDB*, 915–17.

———. "Tabernacles, Feast of." In *WDB*, 921–22.

———. "Temple." In *WDB*, 929–34.

———. "Weeks, Feast of." In *WDB*, 989–90.

Gooding, D. W. "Tabernacle." In *NBD*, 1145–48.

Grimenstein, Edward O. *A Lutheran Primer for Preaching: A Theological and Practical Approach to Sermon Writing*. St. Louis: Concordia, 2015.

Gritsch, Eric W., and Robert W. Jenson. *Lutheranism: The Theological Movement and Its Confessional Writings*. Philadelphia: Fortress, 1976.

Hammer, Joshua. "Finally, the Beauty of France's Chauvet Cave Makes its Grand Public Debut." *Smithsonian Magazine*, April 2015. https://www.smithsonianmag.com/history/france-chauvet-cave-makes-grand-debut-180954582/.

Haselock, Jeremy. "Gestures." In *DLW*, 227–30.

Hymns of Praise. Rev. ed. Hong Kong: Taosheng, 1994.

The International Standard Bible Encyclopedia. Rev. ed. Edited by Geoffrey W. Bromiley et al. Grand Rapids: Eerdmans, 1988.

Jensen, Robin M. *Baptismal Imagery in Early Christianity: Ritual, Visual, and Theological Dimensions*. Grand Rapids: Baker Academic, 2012.

John of Damascus. *On the Divine Images: Three Apologies Against Those Who Attack the Divine Images*. Translated by David Anderson. Crestwood, NY: St. Vladimir's Seminary Press, 1980.

Johnson, Maxwell E. *The Rites of Christian Initiation: Their Evolution and Interpretation*. Rev. exp. ed. Collegeville, MN: Liturgical, 2007.

Johnson, Maxwell E., ed. *Between Memory and Hope: Readings in the Liturgical Year*. Collegeville, MN: Liturgical, 2000.

Justin Martyr. *First Apology*. Translated by Edward Rochie Hardy. Edited by John Baillie et al., 1:242–89. Library of Christian Classics. Philadelphia: Westminster, 1953.

Kane, Thomas A. "Dance, Liturgical." In *DLW*, 150–51.

Kilde, Jeanne Halgren. *When Church Became Theatre: The Transformation of Evangelical Architecture and Worship in Nineteenth-Century America*. Oxford: Oxford University Press, 2002.

Kitchen, K. A. "Burial and Mourning." In *NBD*, 145–50.

Kubicki, Judith Marie. *Liturgical Music as Ritual Symbol: A Case Study of Jacques Berthier's Taizé Music*. Liturgia Condenda 9. Leuven: Peeters, 1999.

Lathrop, Gordon W. *Holy Things: A Liturgical Theology*. Minneapolis: Fortress, 1993.

Levitin, Daniel J. *The World in Six Songs: How the Musical Brain Created Human Nature*. New York: Plume, 2008.

Luther, Martin. *The Annotated Luther*. 6 vols. Edited by Hans Hillerbrand et al. Minneapolis: Fortress, 2015–2017.

———. *Luthers Werke: Kritische Gesamtausgabe [Schriften]*. 65 vols. Weimar: H. Böhlau, 1883–1993.

———. *Luther's Works* [American edition]. Edited by Jaroslav Pelikan et al. 82 vols. planned. Philadelphia: Fortress; St. Louis: Concordia, 1955–86; 2009–.

McGowan, Andrew B. *Ancient Christian Worship: Early Church Practices in Social, Historical, and Theological Perspective*. Grand Rapids: Baker Academic, 2014.

Messerli, Carols R., and Philip Pfatteicher. *Lutheran Book of Worship: Manual on the Liturgy*. Minneapolis: Augsburg, 1979.

Millard, A. R. "Temple." In *NBD*, 1156–59.

Mitchell, Nathan D. *Liturgy and the Social Sciences*. American Essays in Liturgy. Collegeville, MN: Liturgical, 1999.

———. "Rite, Ritual." In *DLW*, 407–10.

Moon, Hwarang. *Engraved Upon the Heart: Children, the Cognitively Challenged, and Liturgy's Influence on Faith Formation*. Eugene, OR: Wipf and Stock, 2015.

Motyer, J. A. "Circumcision." In *NBD*, 204–5.

———. "Prophecy, Prophets." In *NBD*, 964–72.

Music Sourcebook for Lent and the Three Days. Minneapolis: Augsburg Fortress, 2010.

New Bible Dictionary. 3rd ed. Edited by J. D. Douglas et al. Downers Grove, IL: IVP, 1996.

New Dictionary of Theology Historical and Systematic. 2nd ed. Edited by Martin Davie et al. Downers Grove, IL: InterVarsity, 2016.

The New SCM Dictionary of Liturgy and Worship. Edited by Paul F. Bradshaw. London: SCM, 2002.

The New Westminster Dictionary of the Bible. Edited by Henry S. Gehman. Philadelphia: Westminster, 1970.

Newberg, Andrew, et al. *Why God Won't Go Away: Brain Science and the Biology of Belief.* New York: Ballantine, 2001.

Pfeiffer, C. F. "Atonement, Day of." In *NBD*, 104–5.

Rightmire, R. David. "Salvation Army Worship." In *DLW*, 420–22.

Senn, Frank C. *Christian Liturgy: Catholic and Evangelical.* Minneapolis: Fortress, 1997.

———. *Embodied Liturgy: Lessons in Christian Ritual.* Minneapolis: Fortress, 2016.

Stephenson, Barry. *Ritual: A Very Short Introduction.* Oxford: Oxford University Press, 2015.

Stubbes, Philip. *Anatomy of the Abuses in England.* Edited by F. J. Furnivall. New Shakespeare Society Series 6.4 and 6.6. N.p.: Trübner, 1877–79.

Stuempfle, Herman G. *Preaching Law and Gospel.* Ramsey, NJ: Sigler, 1990.

Sturge, Mark. "Black Churches' Worship (United Kingdom)." In *DLW*, 61–62.

Truscott, Jeffrey A. *Sacraments: A Practical Guide.* New Delhi: Christian World Imprints, 2016.

———. *Worship: A Practical Guide.* 2nd ed. Singapore: Genesis, 2020.

Turner, Victor. "Passages, Margins and Poverty: Religious Symbols of *Communitas*." *Worship* 46.8 (1972) 482–94.

———. *The Ritual Process: Structure and Anti-Structure.* New Brunswick, NJ: Aldine Transaction, 2011.

United Methodist Book of Worship. Nashville: United Methodist Publishing House, 1992.

Uzukwu, Elochukwe E. *Worship as Body Language: Introduction to Christian Worship (An African Orientation).* Collegeville, MN: Liturgical, 1997.

Van Gennep, Arnold. *The Rites of Passage.* Translated by Monika B. Vizedom and Gabriele Caffee. Chicago: University of Chicago Press, 1960.

Wallace, R. S. "Calvin, John." In *DTHS*, 143–47.

Wengert, Timothy J. *Word of Life: Introducing Lutheran Hermeneutics.* Minneapolis: Fortress, 2019.

Westerholm, Stephen. "Temple." In *ISBD*, 759–76.

White, James F. *Introduction to Christian Worship.* 3rd ed. Nashville: Abingdon, 2000.

White, James F., and Susan J. White. *Church Architecture: Building and Renovating for Christian Worship.* Akron, OH: Order of St. Luke, 1998.

With One Voice: A Lutheran Resource for Worship. Minneapolis: Augsburg Fortress, 1995.

Wright, J. S., and J. A. Thompson. "Marriage." In *NBD*, 732–36.

Wright, N. T. *Colossians and Philemon.* Tyndale New Testament Commentaries. Grand Rapids: Eerdmans, 1986.

www.ingramcontent.com/pod-product-compliance
Lightning Source LLC
Chambersburg PA
CBHW021827090726
47818CB00077BA/82